RELIGIOUS AMERICA

MCGRAW-HILL BOOK COMPANY   *New York* : *St. Louis* : *San Francisco* : *Dusseldorf* : *London* : *Mexico* : *Sydney* : *Toronto*

Religious America

PHOTOGRAPHS BY PHILIP GARVIN

TEXT BY PHILIP GARVIN AND JULIA WELCH

MCGRAW-HILL BOOK COMPANY

123456789EPDO7987654

Library of Congress Cataloging in Publication Data

Garvin, Philip, 1947–
    Religious America.

    1.   United States — Religious life and customs.
I.   Welch, Julia.   II.   Title.
BR515.G27   209'.73   74-11049
ISBN 0-07-022918- X

Designed by Norman Ives
Typeset by Typographic Art
Printed by Eastern Press.

Author's Note

Religious America started out as a photographic essay supported by the Rockefeller Foundation. I recorded interviews and kept a journal as I traveled throughout the United States from February to September, 1971.

I interrupted that work, briefly, to film the service and people of the Faith Tabernacle Pentecostal church in Riverside, California. Walt Disney Productions generously loaned me the necessary equipment. That film later became the pilot for the TV series which I produced at WGBH-TV, the Boston PBS station and production center. The thirteen-part series was shown nationally on the educational television network. Grants from the Irwin-Sweeney-Miller Foundation, the Corporation for Public Broadcasting, and the Lilly Endowment supported the expensive project. Each program presented one contemporary American congregation, community, or family and always focused on the experiences of individuals.

This book draws from photographs taken during the original eight-month journey, while researching the film subjects, and on subsequent return trips to the films' locations. The photographs in the section on the Hasidic Jews were taken much earlier, in 1967-70.

A few of the photographs were selected from the 260,000 feet of film shot for the TV series. The cameramen were Boyd Estus, Peter Hoving, Nick Doob, Tim Hill, and myself.

Joan Carlson searched the footage for the frames needed for the book. As associate producer of the films, she managed every aspect of the production and participated in the research.

Although the size of the film crew varied from three to eight, Joan, the cameraman, and I were usually complemented by a sound man and assistant cameraman. Unlike some forms of cinema-verité, (where the crew may wait months to capture events), we shot each of the films in seven to nine days. I planned the "on location" schedule during the weeks of research. We spent seven weeks editing the ten hours of film we usually shot into a final 28 minutes.

Fred Hills of the McGraw-Hill Book Company provided the incentive to complete the work, shaping it into a book with sympathetic interest. The very difficult task of designing a book with so many diverse elements was accepted by Norman Ives.

I asked Julia Welch to work with me on the text and edit the transcripts. Her knowledge of the subject, extended travels in the United States, and insight into religious experience made her the only choice.

Most of the photographs are prints from 35mm black and white negatives exposed in Nikons and Pentaxes on TRI-X film, developed in D-76 and Acufine. Several pictures were taken with a view camera on black and white 4″x5″ films. Using internegatives, I converted 35mm slides and 16mm frames into black and white prints.

The prints were made on Kodal Polycontrast F and Agfa Brovira paper by Morris Zeeberg (supervised by Irv Rubin) at the Boris Color Lab in Boston, Massachusetts, by Barbara Dreier of New Haven, Connecticut, and myself.

A work of this scope naturally enlists the cooperation, hospitality, and advice of dozens of people. I am particularly grateful to Sydney Ahlstrom, Howard Elinson, Michael Rice, John Hostetler, Alan Green, Irwin Miller, Card Walker, James Stewart, Charles Williams, Chester La Roche, Norman Lloyd, William Bradley, Jack Biersdorf, Bill Ferris, the Fergusons, Bill Cosel, the Longs, the Luppens, the Martins, the Welchs, the Upshaws, Joan Barkhausen, Mrs. Sherman, the Wrights, Keiko, John Hill, Willabelle Ford, Pauline and Selma Lipsky, Kathy Matthews, Pam Conroy, Liz Van Winkle, Vincent Scully, Linda Cutler, the Hadleys, the Connells, and the Hendersons. Throughout my work, my family has been wonderfully encouraging, always ready with kind words and practical help. I also appreciate WGBH's generosity in permitting the use of verbal and visual material gathered during the making of the film series.

Many of those pictured and quoted in this book have become my good friends. All the people who have shared their personal faith did so knowing that I came to them as a student and admirer. I feel that I have much to learn from these unheralded Americans and I am indebted to them for letting me communicate their vision to others.

PHILIP GARVIN
June, 1974

Contents

Introduction

I had a traveling companion, a wiry black dog named "Charlie," and a second-hand van, painted banana yellow and outfitted with a bed and cabinets. I had also the curiosity and desire for motion that lures young people (and old people) to the open road and across the vast American landscape. In addition, I had acquired two irrelevant degrees from Yale University and some talent in photography. Above all, I had a subject of interest — religion — and therefore a reason to travel: to document the religious experiences of plain, ordinary Americans.

Only a year earlier, when I drove across the United States for the first time, I was certain that American society was consumed by materialism and bereft of religious faith. I was on my way back to New York City from Thailand where I had spent six weeks living in and photographing Buddhist monasteries. The poverty and spirituality of rural Thai society contrasted sharply with what I took to be the characteristic affluent indifference of the United States. The truth is that I was simply ignorant. Except for the intensely devout Hasidic Jews of Brooklyn whom I had photographed for a book, *A People Apart,* I really knew very little about religion in the United States.

Not long after that first cross-country trip I met Phil Welch, a young man who had dropped out of Yale and become a Christian. His example, as well as the information he gave me about the "Jesus movement" and traditional Christianity, encouraged me to think that an exploration of American religion might be a valuable undertaking. When I proposed such a project, the Rockefeller Foundation agreed and promised to finance my work. Charlie and I began our journey in March, 1971.

I planned to document Pentecostals and Mexican-American Catholics in Southern California, Christian communes and monasteries in Northern California, traditional Protestants in the rural Northwest, Catholics in the urban Northwest, Mormons in Utah, Penitentes (Spanish-American Catholics) in New Mexico, Yaqui Indian Catholics in Arizona, black and white Southern Baptists in Mississippi, Holiness Churches in Appalachia, and suburban Lutherans in the Midwest. The immensity of the subject didn't intimidate me. My intent was to focus on individuals rather than institutions, on religious experience rather than religious doctrine. In addition to my four cameras, I brought along a tape recorder to collect interviews.

The toughest part of the work was always the first few hours in a community or at a church. You arrive, a total stranger with only the vaguest idea of what to expect. Awkwardly, you introduce yourself to the pastor, the family, the abbot, or the commune members, and explain that you've come all the way from Connecticut to photograph their personal spiritual lives. Surprise, confusion, amazement, or suspicion ensue. Why me? Why here? The answer to these inevitable questions was always something of a mystery to me as well as to the subjects, but with very few exceptions (like the John Bircher's wife who insisted on "checking me out"), the people I visited always welcomed me into their homes and shared with me their love for God, their strength, and their deepest faith.

In each place the mood was different. Noisy, exuberant Pentecostal prayer meetings contrasted with the unruffled serenity of a day in a monastery. The spirituality of Mississippi black Baptists seemed deep and heavy compared to the bright, buoyant liveliness of the "Jesus people" in the communes I visited. And yet, over and over again, I met a certain kind of person, a man or a woman of faith.

During those eight months on the road, I often suffered from loneliness and boredom. Between one stop and another lay immense distances and hours of monotonous driving highlighted only by occasional hitchhikers, mechanical failures, and food stops. New friends were soon forsaken as I left one community and headed for another. Sometimes it was that very loneliness which compelled me to thrust myself into new experiences and new friendships, to pursue the subjects of my documentation.

Of course, there was Charlie to keep me company. Living for many months in a small van required certain understandings. Charlie learned to urinate on command and patiently tolerated long hours of confinement. He never did give up his favorite diversion — rolling in cow manure — but only once did he chase a skunk. He was an eager and extremely competent fighter with a bite so ferocious that on one occasion I had to pry his mouth open with a tire iron in order to separate him from another dog. No doubt the insecurity of a moving home contributed to his aggressiveness. To me, he was a perfect friend. Five months after we had resettled in the Northeast, Charlie was killed by an automobile.

I never intended, even at the beginning of our travels, to adopt the "objective" pose of a social scientist. Because my spiritual education had been almost nil, I looked forward to the project as an opportunity to open myself up to religious experience. I didn't waste any time. The black Baptists in Los Angeles had me singing my heart out to God on my second day. Two weeks later, I was "slain in the Spirit" by a Pentecostal evangelist. By the time I made it to the Northwest I was giving my testimony. My involvement with photography and religion merged: I remember having trouble finding a darkroom, so I prayed for one and found it right away.

During those first eight months I was strictly concerned with American Christianity. The people I met called me a Christian; my jargon was fundamentalist. But I never lost my admiration for Hasidic and Buddhist spirituality. In time, the three merged into a general notion of religion.

When, unexpectedly, the photographic expedition resulted in a request to produce thirteen films for public television, it was this broad concept of religion which guided me. In choosing the subjects and in making the films for *Religious America,* I tried to illustrate the faith of some people who, through an experience of God, had become what I call "fully human," people who believed and felt that they were part of a whole greater than themselves, and who were in awe of that greatness.

A film crew of five people equipped with 16mm cameras, lights, microphones, tape recorders, and furlongs of extension cord can never be as unobtrusive as a single person with a still camera. Nevertheless, we were able to capture private moments of prayer as well as ecstatic celebrations on film. When devotion was strong, the presence of the crew and the equipment created astonishingly little distraction. At a Hasidic gathering we anchored the camera with heavy weights and still the exuberant dancing rocked it. In Louise, Mississippi, Tommy Taylor, Penny Barnes, and Lizzie Linnear shared their wisdom with the camera as if it were a familiar old friend.

Organizing one hundred and thirty hours of film, fifteen thousand photographs, and dozens of taped interviews into a single volume has inevitably required omissions. What we have selected is certainly not intended to be a comprehensive survey of religion in America, nor is it a diary of my experiences. *Religious America* is a book about people, modest heroes and heroines who are introduced here in the belief that there is something great, something religious about being alive. Working to survive, reproducing, and dying — these are not merely man's lot, but also man's divinity.

RELIGIOUS AMERICA

I Five Communities

San Juan Parish

Having stunned the Rio Grande pueblos into sullen obedience and dispatched his seven Franciscans to perfect their conversion, Don Juan de Oñate, conquistador and colonizer of the New Mexican territory, turned his conqueror's lust inward to the wilderness of his own sins. (So it is conjectured.) Perhaps it was only the hypnotic moonlight which lured him that Good Friday nearly four centuries ago to a spot in the desert where waxy, blood-black, cactus blossoms and pale, leering night lilies bloomed beneath the sage. There he unclothed his upper body and with a whip of yucca and purging aloe began to discipline his flesh. When the soldiers who searched for him (the legend continues) found the illustrious one flaying the skin from his own back and crying out, *"Penitencia!"* to his suffering God, they threw off their tunics and with scourges hastily fashioned from desert thorn, imitated their leader in an orgy of self-punishment, trampling the cool sand, crushing the obscene flowers, and splattering the long-armed ocotillos with red Spanish blood.

The story is told in the shade of Santa Fe patios. Some claim it explains a custom of extreme physical penance which lingers to this day in the remote mountain valleys between the Jemez and San Juan ranges and the Sangre de Christo Mountains. The men who are said to practice it during Holy Week each year, *Los Hermanos en Nuestro Padre Jésus,* are called the "Penitentes."

Of the many rumors surrounding the Penitentes, the most notorious is the most instructive. It holds that their Good Friday penances include not only scourging and fasting, but also the crucifixion of a specially honored brother. Some versions of the story claim the crucifixions are real, others that a man is merely tied to the cross. Neither story is plausible. In spite of repeated contradictions, the rumor persists — perhaps because it illustrates the motive of the secret society: the imitation of Christ in life, in suffering, and (symbolically) in death.

I saw in the window of a gallery in Santa Fe a nineteenth-century Penitente whip — an ugly, barbed *disciplina* of braided metal wire. "Be careful," I was warned. "The Penitentes are very

dangerous. They don't like strangers." Someone gave me the name of a Penitente informant in the town of Truchas: "He *might* tell you something."

Truchas is located on the road between Santa Fe and Taos. The village teeters at the edge of a cliff. Its fissured adobe structures seemed to crouch that day under a low, menacing sky. Erosion had claimed some of them whose decomposing remains could be seen among the talus at the bottom of the precipice. Each sloping yard, scratched bare by chickens, bristled with tilting fences. Dogs whose eyes gleamed with hunger yelped frantically at my approach. Not one person was in sight, but at each of the tiny, misshapen windows a curtain twitched as I drove by.

The man I had come to visit was stupid with fear and suspicion. He was able to tell me nothing, but communicated danger. In Truchas the traditional relationships among members of the Spanish community have been twisted and split by the twentieth century until they have become as disfigured as the blasted junipers that cling to the tops of mesas. The law of the police — "Anglo law" — is worth nothing there. Conflicts end in violence and often in murder.

Abandoning Truchas, I travelled northwest to the remoter villages of San Juan parish. Petaca, La Madera, and Las Tablas are far from a major highway. Tourists do not visit them in overwhelming numbers, nor do the young men of the parish drive into the cities of Taos or Santa Fe each weekend to drink. (They drink at home or at the cafe in Ojo Caliente.) The old people speak a dialect of seventeenth century Spanish, the language of Oñate's settlers and soldiers. They farm the same land granted to their ancestors by the Spanish crown. It is extraordinarily rich land but like some rich men, it conceals its wealth. Where the deep-rooted sage, snakeweed, and Mormon tea grow thin and far apart, water is scanty and far below the surface. Where the sage is thick and tall and overshadowed by piñon, where the thrifty bunch-grass covers the soil, there it rains enough to keep cattle alive. When the rain comes, the effects are spectacular: corn leaps up a foot in height, beans grow fat, and squashes ripen. Orange mallow, scarlet

paintbrush, rusty coneflowers, and crimson pussytoes burst into flame; blue harebells and purple lupine nod in the breezes; birds feast in meadows of wild sunflowers; in the bottoms of arroyos, potent jimsonweed opens its violet blossoms.

It was well-known in the town of Petaca that the leader of the local Penitentes was an old man named Fred. I introduced myself to Fred and explained that I was a student of religion.

"*Sí,* religion," he comprehended and invited me into his house. "Sit down." I took a seat on a rickety chair beside a round, oil-cloth covered table. Faded portraits of saints adorned the cracked walls. The gentle old man fetched up and laid open on the table before me an ancient and profusely illustrated Spanish Bible. In a mixture of Spanish and English, and by pointing a blunt finger at one picture and another, he told me the story of the life of Jesus with digressions on the sacraments of the Catholic faith.

"When I pray," explained Fred, "I feel Jesus, El Niño, in my heart and I see him with eyes of faith." (Behind me, Fred's daughter-in-law whispered, "He means only that he *imagines* these things. Of course he doesn't *see* them.")

"Hell is no burning," the old man continued. "When a man dies he is put in the ground; to be in the grave — that is Hell. The souls wait for resurrection, it is not yet come. From the beginning of the world many wait a long time. When the Judgment comes then it will be decided which ones shall find glory and which shall suffer. I beg the Lord Jesus to take away my sins so that I may live with him and with the angels."

"And do you pray in that building at the edge of town? What is it called?" I asked, pretending to mumble the name of the "Morada" — the windowless, adobe hut where I knew the Penitentes held their vigils.

Old Fred never stopped smiling as he pretended complete ignorance. "Morada? Dorada?" he muttered. "Ah, Dorado Canyon, yes, it is just up the road."

Later I talked to the unofficial "mayor" of Petaca, an important man but not a Penitente. I told him the story of my interview with Fred. Santiago had a good laugh. "What would happen if I simply walked up to the Morada on my own?" I asked him.

"Oh, you would probably get shot," he answered. Then he told me not to get excited. "The Penitentes," he said, "are just like everybody else. They help each other out and mind their own business. But just between you and me, it is too old-fashioned to be like a saint, no? The men nowadays they go all around the world and out into space and even to the moon, and no one yet says he saw the paradise or the inferno."

The next day Father Martinez came to Petaca to say Mass. Santiago, who had told me he always went to church, stayed home and sent his wife to say that he was sick. He was not the only one absent. After the service I introduced myself to the priest, a morose man, about forty years old, who is a native of New Mexico. Martinez is responsible for seven congregations, some of them "backward" and others "corrupted." His facade of dour pessimism belies his total devotion to the parish and love for the Spanish-American people who are, after all, his own brothers and sisters. Martinez invited me to go with him to his next two services. On the way to Las Tablas we discussed the Penitentes.

"The ones who condemn them the most are the ones who understand them the least," he began. "I knew them as I grew up and I know them now. They put to shame those who are ignorant of the meaning of penance. They put it into practice more than so many of us who only put it in books. And really, they have more common sense than to hurt each other in their rites. All these stories about them crucifying each other are rubbish. To me, their practices are simply down-to-earth expressions of faith. They are very beautiful, very sincere, very truthful in their devotion."

Father Martinez explained that the Penitentes became important two centuries ago when the Spanish priests who had roamed the mountains, winning souls and bestowing saintly names on ephemeral missions, suddenly departed. In the remote villages there was no Mass, no communion, no confession, no baptism, not even the sacrament of marriage. But life without God was, and still is,

When I was a little boy, there were many very respectful, strong men in la Morada, in the church all around. Whenever a person died we would mourn for him, wash him, sing for him. Not any more. All of the strong men are gone. Now we have only boys.

My wife who is dead now was a good Catholic, a good person. She never stopped serving God, and was especially devoted to San Antonio, Santo Niño, other saints, too. She adored the miraculous saints. Our house was full of images, full. In these houses nowadays you no longer find pictures of saints, but that's the way we used to be. She was a very Catholic woman.

I also helped in the work of the church, but now nobody does any work, right? Now the people are lost. They don't want to learn, you can't tell them anything. Pleasure is the only thing that matters. New ways, education — everything has changed. Education isn't everything. I didn't have an education but I learned with good faith in the service of God.

Before, the priests were always close to the people. They knew how to reach them, and in their Masses they protected us from evil ways. But now some enter the church in short sleeves. There isn't any respect at all.

I can never abandon all that my wife and I chose to do here. For this reason, I believe that God is in Heaven. I pray to God, asking him to give me good health, to help me through my days. I pray through the saints night and day; I pray to them for the people living here and for the dead; I pray that God might keep them in his glory. And I pray for those who, here on earth, haven't tried to save themselves. There are so many now who go this way and that. I used to know all of the old men here in all of our rites, but now there are no more. All of the real men are gone. Everybody wants pleasure now, only pleasure.

BELARMINO VARÓZ

20

inconceivable for the Spanish-American people. How would the crops and livestock flourish in that dry land; how would there be good hunting without him? In their Moradas, the Penitentes kept the faith alive, sheltered it from apathy, remembered the prayers, and waited for the priests to return. The priests — no longer Spanish, but "American" — returned only to condemn the embroidery of Penitente ritual.

"When I was young," a ninety-year-old Penitente told me, "all the adults belonged to the Morada and they were very, very respectful. They used to see that all the youngsters became good Catholics. Today, it is all changed. Maybe father and mama go to church or perhaps they stay home in bed and sleep late. In those days it wasn't that way. The Moradas were wide open. On Good Friday, all the men used to go in procession from the Morada up to the Calvario where they placed the cross. Two or three followed, whipping themselves. Then a priest came — well, I suppose even the archbishop had something to do with it — and said it was a mockery, that the people were making fools out of themselves. They should do those services more secretly."

Another old man told his version of the story. "Years back," he said, "the priests all over this country got killed. Others were sent back to Old Mexico where they came from. So the people here, they have disbeliefs. That is why they create this association, this little brotherhood, and they went to church, hadn't got no priest but they said the prayers, and if you go and talk to the Bishop, he'll tell you that these brothers are more important than any other association."

In Las Tablas, Father Martinez baptized a little girl. "Celeste," he intoned, "the Christian community welcomes you with great joy. In its name I claim you for Christ our Savior by the sign of this cross." After the service I talked to the child's grandfather, Celestino, outside the church. He pointed to what looked like an abandoned building further up the steep hillside and said with pride, "You see that? That is the Morada where our communal society meets." With remarkable agility, the stooped old man led me up to the Morada and then to a higher spot, the Calvario. The

society's meetings, he explained, were held once a month and, of course, at Eastertime there were "special ceremonies." Neither of us mentioned the word "Penitente."

"Could you tell me what happens in the Morada during the special ceremonies?" I asked.

"Oh, no," he answered politely.

As we bounced and skidded our way toward La Madera, I told Father Martinez about my conversation with Celestino. I expressed surprise that a Penitente would volunteer information, however slight, about his society.

"Up here in these mountains," declared Martinez, "the people are not ashamed of their piety. And here the anthropologists and tourists leave them alone; they are not influenced by other cultures. You will see in La Madera, the people are proud of their heritage."

La Madera is a larger village than Petaca or Las Tablas. Earth-brown adobe houses, timbered with weathered pine, line both sides of the "main street," a paved section of the county road. Unemployed young men, bored by idleness, lounge on the porch of the combination post office, gas station, and general store. They sip Dr. Peppers while they wait to tip their straw cowboy hats and flash brilliant smiles at every young woman who passes by. In the center of the town is the church and behind it the cemetery where the ancestors are buried, but not forgotten.

During Holy Week, 1971, Father Martinez said a Mass for the first time in the "Oratorio" in La Madera. The Oratorio is the building adjacent to the Morada where the Penitentes conduct the parts of their ceremonies that are open to all the townspeople. Penitente and non-Penitente alike were filled with pride because he honored the brotherhood so highly.

"All the people were surprised to see our Father for the first time give us the Mass up there," recalled Frank Gallegos, a fifty-year-old Penitente. "He was very happy to do that for us, our brotherhood, and it brought us more interest in our membership. The people enjoyed our small church and that is what we are proud of."

Gallegos spoke with that unaffected softness and tranquillity characteristic of men of great strength and self-discipline. His humility seemed to extend far beyond the common deference rural Spanish-Americans display toward strangers. His manner suggested the conviction one senses in a man who has made vows of deep commitment.

"What we do up there in the Morada," he continued, "it is my duty to let people know. Our neighbors who have been raised in this country hereabouts, they used to know these rites and here in La Madera the faith is still strong. We pray up there, we try to help our people, and to help the church in our community. Our enemies, we pray for them also so that our God will forgive their sins. We pray for all the living and also for the dead — our fathers and mothers, all the people who were born here and died here, we never forget to pray for them."

Later I talked to Charles Gallegos, Frank's sixteen-year-old nephew. He spoke slowly and thoughtfully. "I've thought about joining," he said. "I've heard some stories about the whipping, about taking the same punishment Jesus took. My cousin told me that if you peek in the window of the Morada you can see blood splashed on the walls."

"What happens if they catch you spying on them?" I asked.

"If you get caught, they give you the same punishment they take themselves, I guess. So I haven't dared to go see."

"And if you fear the punishment, why would you want to join the brotherhood?"

Charles considered his answer before replying with signs of agitation: "Well, it is something a good man should do for Jesus. He did so much for us, he suffered and he died. He helps us all the time, in all things, all our lives. My uncle told me, 'If you want to do something extra for God, join. If you don't, you'd better not. Religion isn't meant to be easy.' "

Father Martinez told me later, "You cannot say they go to extremes because they do this out of love for Christ and when you do something out of love, you can't do anything too extreme."

On Holy Thursday in 1972 I returned to La Madera to hear Father Martinez say Mass in the Oratorio. The service was held in the evening in the tiny adobe building on the mountainside a mile outside town. A few pictures of the crucified Jesus hung on the whitewashed, plaster walls, dimly visible in the light of kerosene lamps. The ceiling was low and smoke-blackened. At one end of the room, white cloths had been draped over a long bench. On this makeshift altar had been placed candles, a cross, and the communion vessels. The worshippers who filled the room were mostly women and children. Martinez entered, his expression more stern and gloomy than ever, and made his way silently to the altar. Only then did the Penitentes, about thirty in number, march two-by-two down to the Oratorio from the Morada. They moved slowly like blind men and with the same uncanny sureness. The audience avoided their stony eyes. When the Mass ended, the Penitentes returned to the Morada, there to continue until Easter morning whatever secret penances their vigil includes. As the door of the Morada shut behind the procession of brothers, extinguishing the last gleam of light on that dark, sage-mottled slope, my curiosity died away. Every feature of the landscape began to seem grotesquely animate. I was seized by a feeling of panicky vulnerability, that sense of being watched and inexorably surrounded by someone else's ancestors which sometimes overwhelms the city-dweller who strays upon the land.

I hurried back to my rented car and fearing, for some reason, to turn on the headlights, drove in the moonlight down the mountain toward the town. The dirt track followed the course of a tiny river; its hard-baked surface gleamed like metal in the frozen light. I imagined the path flowing in obedience to the same laws as the rivulet's down to a wider, graded channel of gravel, down again to the pavement of the county road, thence to the valley and the four-lane concrete highway, and on toward the golden lights of Sante Fe. I pictured myself in the company of turquoise-laden heiresses listening to a conversation on Spanish-American folklore. Between the Morada and the capital city, the space seemed insignificant: the length of a silver ribbon. In fact, the gap was far greater, a distance of centuries.

St. James' Church

We're trying to get ourselves out of the way and be channels of God's life which is the only true life and the only true harmony and order in the universe. We just try to be open to God's marvelous river of life. And to pass it on. I mean, that's what loving is. As soon as you keep it, it gets stale and stagnant and you become like the branch that Jesus talked about that has been broken off and is withered and of no use. But when you pass it on, the life flows through you and gives life to others and yourself. That's a really joyful thing.

A MEMBER OF ST. JAMES' DEVOTIONAL GROUP

"I must admit that it's far easier, particularly for a career woman, to stay home in bed Sunday morning," Joan Watters told me, straightening her silver necklace as we began the interview, "but going to church on Sunday is part of my strict discipline. Friends ask, 'How can you get up and go to church every single Sunday?' They think perhaps I'm a little bit unusual. I wouldn't dare tell them how I pray or read my Bible every day. Some people feel that it's a crutch and I have often wondered if perhaps that's true. If so, it's a pretty good one. It certainly works for me."

Few of Joan Watters' friends knew the strength of her faith in God until they heard her speak of it on television in a film we made about St. James' Church, an Episcopal Church on Madison Avenue, and its wealthy, well-educated congregation. The spiritual life of a sophisticated New Yorker is a private matter, not a topic of casual conversation as it is for the people of Knapp, Minnesota or Louise, Mississippi. After the film aired, many of Joan's acquaintances remarked, "I didn't know you were *that* way. Tell me about it . . ."

Two weeks before Christmas, when we had the taxi strike in New York and the sidewalks were so crowded, I was down on 43rd and Lexington, practically across the street from Grand Central. It was a beehive down there. I was walking along on my way to an appointment and all of a sudden I felt someone take me by the arm and push me up against the side of a building. I looked up and there was this tall man with a beard and chains all around his neck with a great big peace symbol. And he had something pressed right here, against my side, and I heard him say, "Give me everything you have or I'll kill you." I just couldn't believe it. I said to him, "You mean, you'd kill me here in front of all these people?" And he said, "Listen, lady" (this happened to be on a Wednesday), he said, "I haven't eaten since Saturday. The only way you get things in this world is by force." And so naturally I gave him everything I had and then as he went away he said, "God bless you." And I found myself saying "God bless you" right back to him. It seemed strange, you know, but then it also seemed quite natural. God gives us the strength to love.

JOAN WATTERS

Slowly, quiet Christians like Joan have begun to share the meaning of their faith with others. "Yes, I do pray, I rely on God," many have admitted. Faith in God has come to seem more relevant and necessary as the pressures of urban life become heavier.

St. James' parishioners eagerly describe the church's changing role in the community. Impelled by a sense of Christian duty and by compassion for the less fortunate, concerned members of the congregation participate in numerous social welfare programs. Some visit prisoners in the city's jails. Others who are unable to contribute labor, give financial support to tutoring projects or drug rehabilitation centers. If they were asked about the growth of the church, most members would cite these outreach programs, with good reason, as examples of progress toward more meaningful Christianity.

Fewer are likely to mention the delicate unmasking of spiritual convictions that is subtly transforming St. James'. Evidence for this transformation comes from the men and women of St. James' "devotional group" who meet weekly to study and pray together, and to share each other's concerns.

"When we began we were quite stiff and orderly," recalled one of the founders. "Someone sat at the end of the room; we all sat in straight chairs. We followed a strict program and I'd say that prayer was the lesser part of it and study was the larger amount. We were shy at first. And then as time went on it was very interesting to see more and more of a demand for silent and vocal prayer together."

"It gives us great strength to know that there are other people very much like ourselves who pray the same way," explained another enthusiastic member of the group. "We don't feel embarrassed about it and don't mind talking about it. Our faith is strengthened by sharing it with one another. I know from being in this group that I've learned to love better."

One woman said, "By praying for others and sharing our troubles with the group, our personal problems somehow fall away. The support, the loving concern which we know is always here in the group helps us solve our problems."

Though small, the group is influential in the church. One of their concerns has been to pray for the healing of spiritually and physically afflicted members of the congregation. When they requested a service with the traditional laying on of hands, a seldom-performed healing ceremony of the Episcopal church, Dr. Coburn, the rector, responded enthusiastically. There are now two of the special services a month.

"I'll never forget the first laying-on-of-hands service I participated in," said Almus Thorpe, a young minister of the church. "It was as new to me as it was to many of the people in the congregation. They came up and offered before the Lord their concerns and their needs — either for themselves or for others — and trusted me as a representative, a minister of God through Jesus Christ, to lay my hands upon their heads and to impart to them through prayer his strengthening spirit. It moved me greatly and I'm sure it moved others."

The laying-on-of-hands service is held during the middle of the week and attracts only a few dozen participants. No one has criticized it. More controversial have been changes introduced in one of the two Sunday morning services, changes whose intent is to encourage spontaneity and involve the staid congregation in a more festive celebration.

Until recently, both services were formal and elegant. A well-rehearsed choir performed baroque hymns to the accompaniment of a large and mellow organ; the rector offered a timely, witty sermon; Holy Communion was served with reverent ceremony. Except for insignificant, well-bred rustlings (a slender, small-boned woman hushing the naughty scion of a banking establishment; a portly gentleman stooping to retrieve a lady's glove), the audience was silent and attentive. Dignity, poise, and reserve, not effervescence, distinguished the parishioners' attitudes.

The thaw came slowly. The same voices that praised St. James' progress in assisting the underprivileged at first deplored experimental singing and dancing in the church and disapproved of innovations in the ceremony of Holy Communion which assigned to the formerly passive recipients an active role in sharing the bread

and wine among their fellow communicants. Traditionalists held these changes to be affronts to the dignity of worship and lamented the distressing intimacy such participation imposed.

Although some persist in their criticisms (and attend a later service), many of the dubious ones have become enthusiastic. Officers of banks and insurance companies, board chairmen, and advertising executives have begun attending seminars in "personal religion" offered by Dr. Coburn after the Sunday service. They have dared to return to that simple faith and trust in God which many of them have neglected since childhood, and they are learning that investing this faith in others increases its value. Stodgy Bible lessons and lectures on church doctrine formerly constituted the church's adult education program; these have been replaced by discussion groups and workshops in which members are encouraged to act out the spiritual drama of their lives. Rising church attendance is the ultimate testimony to the success of the movement which, some argue, is not a new advance but a beneficial retreat to 'historic practices of the Anglican Church.

Best of all, Joan maintains, is the openness many of the parishioners have learned to display toward one another. Among those who once considered it vulgar or indiscreet to discuss one's personal problems or doubts with others, there is now a realization that self-reliance is as futile as trust is necessary. The church offers friendship, and those who have accepted it have grown to depend on the support of fellow worshippers and to rely on God-given strength through prayer. That one is not alone in this world is not always self-evident; it is a fact that is discovered with relief.

"Sometimes it is painful to face modern-day life," Joan admits, "and it is awfully nice to know that there is somebody whom you love and who loves you. I could not jump a single hurdle in my life without the knowledge and love of God. He gives me considerable strength, the strength you need to live in New York City. I can walk down the streets and despite the horns honking and all the noises of the city, find peace in my prayers to God. He gives me tranquillity and the courage to face any situation life might offer."

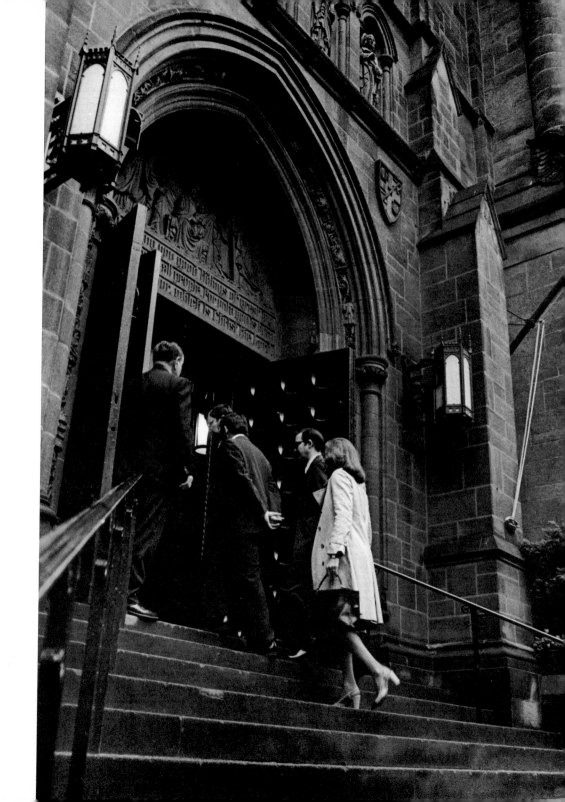

I don't think of religion in a narrow sense. I have tasks and commitments as a mother, as a wife, as a lover, as a teacher. They're all religious tasks. And I am fulfilling my religious commitment by doing the best job in each of those areas that I possibly can. This quest to do right by yourself in all of the things that make a difference in life, it's essentially religious.

JOANNE THORPE

The thing that is so great about the church at this moment is that it speaks of love. I don't hear anyone else talking about it much. I don't hear politicians talking about it. I don't hear the government talking about it. Other people are busy talking about other things, other aspects of life. The church is the one persistent voice that concerns itself with love, with caring about other people.

DICK MULLENS

33

Koinonia

One night in December, 1972, a dozen typewriters were stolen from the basement of the Koinonia Missionary Baptist Church in Gary, Indiana. That a church might be robbed came as a surprise to no one in Gary, but the theft caused the congregation two-fold dismay. Not only did it lose its investment in the expensive machines, but it was compelled to halt part of its new job training program as well.

The next evening two young men strolled into the church and asked to speak privately with Reverend Brown, the pastor. "What's this mean, this 'Koinonia?' " they asked him. "It's Greek. It means 'community,' " Reverend Brown explained. "Oh, yeah?"

The young men had heard that Reverend Brown was "different" and that his church was different, too. Koinonia "did things for the brothers and sisters." The two youths listened intently as Brown, a former Freedom Rider and a seasoned activist, talked about building black manhood and described some of the church's projects in political education, drug rehabilitation, job training, and self-defense.

"We're trying to develop revolutionaries," Brown told them. "Revolutionaries who understand the message of Jesus Christ. Because any system that puts down people, Jesus spoke against. We're trying to teach people how to be that type of revolutionary, how to speak against oppression and put the oppressors down."

The young men approved Brown's message. As they got up to leave, one of them asked, "Are you missing some typewriters?" Brown said he was. "How soon can you pick them up?" "Right away," Brown answered. The young man named a corner in a deserted neighborhood. "Be ready with a truck in fifteen minutes," he suggested.

The next day the typewriters were back on their stands; the secretarial skills class continued its lessons. "I don't think this could have happened anywhere else in Gary," Brown said. "The community is willing to trust us and to protect its programs."

"Our church and the community have a reciprocal relationship," explained one of Koinonia's members. "The community needs us and we need the community." The church was founded in 1971 by a handful of middle-aged, middle-class blacks who, despite their conservative language and appearance, shared a radical conviction that the problems of unemployment, crime, drug abuse, poverty, and ill-health in the black community were in part their responsibility. The traditional churches offered them little but a place to pray for the needy and to give hearty thanks to God for their own good fortune. The words of the Gospels and the teachings of Martin Luther King convinced them that these were merely puny gestures. To be fulfilled as Christians, it was necessary to apply the lessons of brotherhood, to put faith into action, and to follow the calling to serve their least fortunate neighbors.

During his years with the Student Non-violent Coordinating Committee and the Southern Christian Leadership Conference, "Red" Brown had developed a similar conviction that a Christian must be a "suffering servant" of the people. He had also learned how to "organize." Koinonia's founders persuaded Brown to lead their effort and formed a new church whose intention was "to get God out of the church and into the community." The congregation now numbers over three hundred. Hundreds more are involved in its outreach programs, health care projects, karate classes, and adult-education workshops. None of the newcomers is ever urged to go "upstairs" to a religious service or to accept formal membership in the church. Koinonia's leaders see no difference between spiritual

We have a band called "BUS" for "Black Uprising Sound." We rehearse over at the Koinonia center. Eventually I went over to the Sunday service at Koinonia and I really liked it. Reverend Brown was for real. What he was saying was down to earth. He wasn't just talking because he was the preacher — he seemed like a God-sent man.

Koinonia is not a front. Since we've been playing there our gigs have increased and Reverend Brown has helped us get credit to buy our equipment. Before we touch our instruments, before we play anywhere, we always say a prayer and thank the Lord for getting us where we are and making us what we are right now. If we're successful, ten percent of everything we make will go back to Koinonia church to use for the development of programs here in the city — like recording studios.

JEFF LUCAS

needs and worldly needs; their goal is to build pride and self-satisfaction in their brothers and sisters in whatever way they can.

Supporting the church are dedicated Christians like Millie Jones. "Before Koinonia, I would go to church and come back home and still feel a void," she recalled. "Something was missing. When I heard about the Koinonia idea of fellowship in the community, with the whole community participating, I knew that was just what I needed."

Mrs. Jones is heroically modest and generous. She was absolutely hostile to the idea that she might be somebody special. Like so many of the people I filmed for the television series, she was astounded that "anybody'd want to waste their time on me." When I insisted that I thought she was a remarkable person, she simply snorted in disbelief. She glowered at me more ferociously each time I expressed my admiration for her. Mrs. Jones gave her interpretation of the Koinonia ideal:

"It's nice to come to church and worship and sing and praise God, but what he really wants us to do is to serve, to praise, to honor and love one another. That's the way we should serve him. God wants everybody to know about him and he has no tongue but our tongues, no feet but our feet, so he expects us to go and tell the good news to everybody, everywhere."

Mrs. Jones' job as a registered nurse in an intensive care unit is a demanding one, but it is only part of her day's work. Her "spare" hours are filled with activities at the church: preparing hot lunches, practicing with the choir, attending evening prayer meetings. On Sunday mornings she leads a prayer and song service for the patients of a local geriatric center. Mrs. Jones believes that she needs to serve the isolated, forgotten people who inhabit the center as much as they need her kind attention and prayers.

"Have you ever had the beautiful experience of giving something to somebody that they really need?" she asked the old people one Sunday morning. "I believe that everybody needs love. How would you feel if you woke up in the morning and thought that nobody cared about you? If your nurse didn't come in the morning . . . if you woke up and the person next to you didn't say good

There's nothing important about my life. I'm one person the Lord made. Do you think you're important? You know, you may be a millionaire but you're still just a man. God doesn't love you any more because you're older or richer than I am or because you say you've been a Christian for twenty years and I just became one today. If most of us really took time to evaluate ourselves and examine our fears, we would probably answer: there's nothing about me that's all so special or important. I am somebody because the Lord made me.

MILLIE JONES

You may not have a bed to sleep in, maybe you don't even have food for your next meal, but you're a man because God made you that way and no human being can change that. There are no inferiors and superiors, no big I's and little you's. A man is a man because God created him a man. If you believe that, you'll be able to go ahead and do the things the Lord expects a man to do.

REVEREND BROWN

morning . . . We need to develop our talent for love, and never let it go unnoticed, unattended. There is a part of God in all of us and for that reason alone we should be able to keep on loving. That's something nobody can take away from us.

"Thank you so much for coming out this morning," she added. "You know, each time I leave you, I feel so uplifted. You've done so much for me."

The patients marvel. Accustomed as they are to being treated as useless, expendable burdens, these simple words are treasures to be hoarded through the week. The repetition of them flavors the insipid, starchy food, shortens the intolerably dull hours of daytime television, and fills the vacuum of insomniac nights.

The Koinonia congregation knows that in order to strengthen the spirit of the community, they must first build the self-esteem of its members. To the old people, to drug addicts, to ex-convicts, to children, and to all their brothers and sisters, the members of the church carry the message: you are made in the image of God.

"We have a saying, 'everybody is somebody,' " Reverend Brown explained. "No matter what his color, no matter who he is, a man's made in the image of God. And because he's in that image, he is somebody. It's up to those of us who know who we are to help our brother affirm who he is. We must give that brother a firm hand."

When childhood ends (and it usually ends early), street life begins for many black youths in Gary. On the street, hope gives way rapidly to hatred and despair; alcoholism, drug addiction, prison, or death too often follow. Reverend Brown and his followers try to stem this waste of lives by offering alternatives: job training provides the hope of employment; political education suggests methods of dealing with oppression; and karate classes teach not only self-defense, but self-control and self-confidence.

As he watched a karate class perform its drills and listened to the students' menacing grunts and chilling howls, Brown described his conception of the God in whose image man is made:

"When I study Jesus," he said, "I see the man in him. I recognize the God in him, but I understand him as a man and a liberator — a liberator of the oppressed. I understand him as a rugged person, not as the very humble, feminine looking thing that we see all the time in pictures. I understand him in a way that helps me affirm my manhood and I try to live as closely as I can to him.

"A man is one who has a purpose, has objectives, and at the same time is a liberator," he continued. "A man has to be ready to lay down his life for his brother if he wants to understand the Kingdom, if he wants to understand picking up and bearing the cross. That's what the cross is all about. A lot of people lay around the cross, but very few people want to pick up the cross. But a man does all this out of an understanding of Jesus Christ. Love becomes his motivation and Jesus becomes his ideal."

After a week of hard work, the Koinonia congregation assembled in church. ("The church is the altar of celebration," explains Brown. "From eleven to one on Sunday we celebrate and enjoy all the things we've done for our brothers and sisters during the week, works of mission inspired by Jesus.") The celebration was like any traditional black Baptist service. The deacons took their seats in the front of the church; a spirited soloist led the choir in "Amazing Grace"; enthusiastic interjections punctuated Brown's announcements of events of the past week and the week to come. What distinguished Koinonia's worship service from those of traditional churches was the congregation's obvious sense of accomplishment, their joy in the knowledge that they have given what Millie Jones calls "service and substance." Reverend Brown prayed for the energy to work even harder and offered his message:

"Too long have we fought skirmishes in the battle of will, too long have we raised our fists at the corporate and political giants of society, too long have we done all these things without God, without the power of our heavenly Father whose power is like that of a rolling stone. This morning then, I want you to understand that yes, we must be free. Yes, we must have dignity. Yes, we must be liberators, not just of the oppressed but for the oppressors, but this will never be until we accept God as our source of power. This morning I want you to reach out and touch somebody. Touch somebody if you can. Lord, give us clean hearts so that we may be used by Jesus. Let us reach out and touch. Lord, give us clean hearts."

Old Plaza Church

The missions of San Juan Parish were over two centuries old when Spanish Franciscan fathers said their first Mass at the Church of Our Lady Queen of Angels in the small village which became Los Angeles. Old Plaza Church, as it is called more often today, is the oldest Catholic church in California. Since its founding in 1812, thousands of Spanish-speaking Americans have been baptized, confirmed, and wedded in the church and, before dying, seen their children and grandchildren baptized there also. The toothless old men who sit ravelling their knotty fingers next to mute, placid wives, have heard countless Masses, said innumerable rosaries, and watched more than one slim priest become a stout bishop.

The church is never empty. Between Masses a penitent may kneel in one of the alcoves and plead for mercy before the statue of a saint. Silent, veiled women pause in the entrance to dab the holy water, then tiptoe to the chapel to light candles. Unseen lips murmur syllables of prayer which escape the vast shadows and ascend like sluggish bubbles to the vaulted ceiling. At the confessional, a discreetly carved door edges open, revealing the black skirts of a priest, then, closing again, becomes invisible.

Today most of the congregation are Mexican-Americans whose folk traditions are quite different from those of San Juan Parish. Old Plaza's Spanish-speaking priests are sympathetic to their desire for a warm, colorful church which "keeps up the old ways."

During Holy Week each year, Old Plaza Church becomes the

I approach the resurrection on my own intellectual level and on my own emotional level, and yet it has to be basically a matter of faith. Because if you are living only on emotions, then it can be here today and gone tomorrow. And yet the resurrection is not here today and gone tomorrow — it is a constant thing.

FATHER GONZALES

During Holy Week I live deeply all the mysteries of our religion, especially the main one which is the resurrection. The spirit of the resurrection is for me like the moment when a big cloud that is covering the sun all of a sudden moves away, and the beautiful sunshine pours down brilliantly, brilliantly, filling everything with light and gladness.

ENRIQUE SILVA

The resurrection, to me, is like the birth of my first child. In anticipation and waiting you live until there comes the pain of the birth itself. It is vivid like the passion Christ endured, but the joy is so tremendous when, at last, the child is born that everything else becomes shadowy in comparison. We don't forget God's pain or his death on the cross, but these fade away in the glory of his resurrection.

ISABELLA SILVA

42

setting for an emotional and elaborate reenactment of Christ's passion and his resurrection. Anticipation begins on Palm Sunday when the triumph of the Mass is tinged with foreboding. A long service in the evening on Holy Thursday celebrates the memory of the Last Supper. Devout worshippers come and go, each offering thanks with joy that on this last night among his disciples, Jesus bestowed upon Christians of all ages the gift of Holy Communion. The joy is short-lived. Tonight, they remember, will come the betrayal and then the inevitable Passion.

The next evening spectators flood the streets near the church. They come from all over the city and from the suburbs to see the Old Plaza's Good Friday procession. Priests stand in the middle of intersections and coax uncooperative Los Angeles drivers to yield to the parade of bright costumes and painted statues. Dozens of little angels march by dressed in gold, followed by men robed as Roman soldiers and women playing the parts of Mary Magdalene, Santa Veronica, and other saints favored by Mexicans. But the mood is somber. One man portrays Jesus. He wears a crown of thorns and carries a massive cross. He stumbles dramatically as the soldiers goad him on.

The procession ends at the church. Inside, an enormous throng of mourners waits in line to kiss a glass coffin. In the coffin lies an effigy of the dead Jesus. The agony of loss fills the imaginations of the worshippers.

"He has just died an hour or so ago," one man explained. "Then you kneel down and kiss the coffin. To kiss the coffin when Christ is dead, that is a moment of sorrow and also love. He died for us and that is a beautiful thing. It gives a great feeling of love for him."

After the crucifixion, the mood of Holy Week changes from grief to expectation. On Holy Saturday, the waiting is made lively by the performance of an old Mexican ceremony called the "Blessing of the Animals."

"I remember it from my childhood," recalled a man born in Mexico. "When I was young I always brought a little cat or maybe a little dog to the priest for the blessing. It is done so the animals

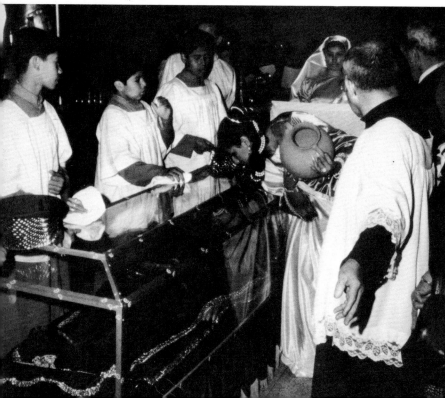

will be preserved from sickness, produce more, and be a help to man."

Years ago when the church's parishioners were farmers, they brought horses, cows, mules, and oxen to the church plaza to be blessed. Now beribboned cats and dogs, rabbits, and more exotic pets are part of the festivity. Their magenta, turquoise, and scarlet clad owners parade them by the priests to the percussion of guitars and maracas. Skillful terriers prance on two legs while highstrung poodles endeavor to slip from their rhinestone collars. Glittering vaqueros clatter by on silver-spangled horses. One awestruck child clutched a monstrous and uncaring turtle which she lifted solemnly toward the priests for a sprinkling of holy water.

On Easter Sunday, the celebration of Christ's resurrection begins at dawn. One joyful Mass follows another until the end of the day as thousands of worshippers flock to the church. Women wrapped in their most gorgeous shawls and finest lace hold twinkling crosses and rosaries, while children, splendid and starchy in white shirts and dresses, make their First Communion. On this day the concentric miracles are united: daily Eucharist, annual rebirth, and eternal life. The Spanish Mass proclaims:

This is the sacrament of our faith.
We announce your death.
We proclaim your resurrection.
Come, Lord Jesus.

The odor of lilies lingers in the church after the last worshipper has gone home to feast. Many members of the congregation live in distant suburbs, far from the church and in other Catholic parishes. Nevertheless, they will return the next Sunday and every other Sunday to hear the Mass at Old Plaza. Father Gonzales, head pastor of the church, explained their faithfulness:

"For the Spanish-speaking person, no matter how crowded it might be, how hot or how small, the church is always a home. Home is something very special. Home has warmth and music, a father and a mother. Home has so many things that you cannot define but you can feel. And this is why the people come to the Old Plaza Church. Because it is home."

44

I feel there is something within me that helps me strive. That faith helps us to feel that a piece of bread is the body of Christ and the wine in the chalice is his blood. And he has said, everyone who eats of this bread and drinks up this cup, proclaims my death. And everyone who eats my bread or my body and drinks my blood will have eternal life. And I believe that.

I remember the death of my mother. I felt sorrow when she died a long time ago and I'm still feeling sorrow. This sadness, Christ's death, is the same. Christ is alive after two thousand years because we still feel all the things he did for us as if it were yesterday.

ENRIQUE SILVA

45

Crow River Christmas, 1972

Farmers have a partnership with God, you know. We plant the seed and without the rain and the sunshine God gives us, why we wouldn't get any crop. I think we realize that, although we probably don't think about it enough. The Scripture says God lets it rain on the just and the unjust. I think, whether or not I'm a Christian or go to church or whatever, we'd still have rain and crops. What I like to do is to give the Lord praise for the rain and crops we do get, and thank him for it. Back there in the thirties when it didn't rain and we got dust storms, whether it was Christians or non-Christians didn't matter. We didn't have any crops; we had to sell our cattle. Couldn't get feed for them or hay, but I don't think we blamed God for not providing us with rain. He was still our savior and the one we had to depend on.

ART CHRISTENSON

"My grandfather and my uncle and one aunt left Sweden in the summer of eighteen hundred and sixty-eight," Art Christenson told me as he arranged his stool and milk pail beside a docile Guernsey. "I don't know exactly how long they spent on the water but it took several weeks to get across. And the food was bad, the bread got moldly — but that's the way they did it back in those days."

The milk hissed into the pail. It was thin and discolored because the cow had just calved. For this reason, Art milked her separately and by hand. The sweetness of cud and of moist manure mingled with the steamy breath of the animals and saturated the atmosphere of the barn.

"They came up here and bought this piece of land where we are now," Art continued. "They built a log house right out here and that's where I was born."

Art has spent most of his eighty years on the farm in Knapp, Minnesota. His arch-roofed barn and his silos, close by the white clapboard farmhouse, are surrounded by neat rectangles of undulating pasture and crop land, planted in summer in alfalfa, feed corn, or beans. At the boundaries of his acreage begin the glacier-billowed fields of neighbors' farms. Visible above the receding

God controls the elements, the wind, the waves, and the powers in nature, but he is also a God who is very close to us and to whom we can speak in prayer. I talked to God this morning. I asked him to lead and guide me throughout this day. I asked him to cleanse my heart and forgive my sins. I'm so glad that we can come freely up to the Lord in prayer.

PASTOR LEE

I was brought up in the country in a Christian home. I remember how my father read his Bible; it was tattered and worn when he passed away. When I read parts of the Scriptures nowadays and hear folks talk about them, I remember: Daddy read that, Daddy spoke about that. It didn't mean to me then nearly what it means to me now, but I sure am thankful I heard it when I was a child.

MRS. LEE

hummocks like the masts of distant sailing vessels are other silos and barn roofs and occasional windmills until at last the fleet vanishes at the horizon.

"It's always been a good community," Art recalled as he stripped the last drops of milk from the cow. "People have always gotten along real well together. They were mostly Scandinavians, you know. They met here and got to know each other and the first thing they thought about after getting their homes built was to found a church, a place where they could go to sing praises to the Lord."

The crossing of two section roads defines the center of Knapp township. There stands the North Crow River Lutheran Church. Its shingled steeple rises above the trees, higher than any silo or any windmill. At the same corner is the Knapp general store; in front of it, two rust-flaked gasoline pumps. There is no other church, no other store, no other variation in the agricultural landscape. At the store, farm neighbors greet each other with bits of innocent gossip and inquire by name after each other's sons and daughters, the absent ones who are raising grandchildren in distant cities. From an estate of rural memories, this new generation will inherit only nostalgia. ("So many move away," says Art. "We had nine children and only two remain now in the church here.")

On Sunday morning the same neighbors meet at the church. The men wear white shirts and string ties under their work-day mackinaws; the women protect their dressy shoes with rubber galoshes. After the simple service they pursue the topics of week-day conversations: new recipes, new fertilizers, the weather, the war in Vietnam. "Will your boys be home for Christmas? And Dorothy with the new baby?"

Art returned the cow from the stanchion to her pen, cleaned his milk pail, and led me across the yard to the house. The winter of 1972 came late in Minnesota. In the fields, corn stubble poked through the shrunken remains of one light snow. The hazy sky gave only a vague hope of a white Christmas. (Children examined it in suspense.)

49

We scuffed the mud and ice off our boots before we stepped into Mrs. Christenson's kitchen. The fragrance of cardamom and citron, ginger and almond poured out of her oven; Christmas savouries simmered on the stove. Potato sausages were ready for the family dinner. Stored safely away from modern noses was the malodorous "lutfiske" that so delights the old folks.

In other kitchens of Knapp there were similar preparations and extravagant consumptions of butter, cream, and eggs. Children washed and dried red-glass condiment dishes and laid out holly-printed napkins around expanded dinner tables. Nougats, pepper-mints, and ribbon candy were arranged in silver dishes and set by centerpieces made of pine cones and painted wooden mushrooms. Other small fingers busied themselves costuming gingerbread men with silver dragées and a motley of colored sugar crystals.

The pastor and his family went out to chop down a Christmas tree. From the attics of Knapp were brought down dusty boxes of old, brittle ornaments, each wrapped carefully in last year's crepe paper and foil. Fancy bows and ribbons, "too pretty to throw away," were found to have slipped to the bottom of the crates and become lopsided, wilted, and faintly acid-smelling. Little League victories, summer vacations, or new fall clothes had obscured, as every year, a vivid recollection of the Christmas treasures. Thus a fleeting, guilty sensation of disloyalty enhanced the children's joyful reunion with the glass balls which spelled their names in glitter, brought back from Minneapolis as souvenirs of Santaland; the angels who revolved above candles and made golden bells tinkle; the venerable, hand-carved reindeer, made in the old country and now deficient in antlers, who had to be placed gently and reverently on the mantelpiece and tilted against the wall in order to spare his bandaged hoof.

All these were unpacked in one house or another as the time drew near to celebrate Christ's birth. Neighbors travelled from farm to farm exchanging Christmas cookies for fresh-baked Julekakes. Christmas carollers sang at each other's doorsteps and filled their pockets with cookies and sweets. The church choir held one last rehearsal as the decorations committee finished decking the church with poinsettias and holly branches and holiday candles.

Mrs. Christenson poured us coffee as we sat at her big kitchen table. Art warmed his fingers against the thick mug. "In the old days," he reminisced, "we didn't have an automobile to ride in to Sunday school. We walked all the way, three miles I guess it was. We'd walk across the fields where there were trails every Sunday, over and back, unless the weather was too bad. And I remember at Christmas time, fifty, sixty years ago, seeing people who didn't go to church all year. They'd come walking by the farm from west of here, probably three or four miles, and they'd walk as far as North Crow River Church to listen to the Christmas story on Christmas morning. We'd all get up and walk to the service at six o'clock and sometimes there'd be a foot of new snow and we'd wade through that snow down there to the church. We'd take turns breaking trail and there'd be probably thirty or forty people when we got as far as Knapp. You see there was something about Christmas that brought people who didn't come to church all year. Something attracted them and it was the birth of the Christ child, I'm sure."

"We call him the 'prince of peace.' He was born to bring peace into the world, but it seems the world is never at peace. There is one thing that is happening now that spoils the Christmas season for many people. I hear they escalated the war over there in Vietnam. Now they're dropping more bombs than ever — 20,000 tons just yesterday — and they're falling on human beings like ourselves, human beings created by God, our Father. That's the way the world is. We forget about the prince of peace and his promises and what he asked us to do, told us to do, to love one another. He said, you shall love the Lord your God above all things and you should love your neighbor as yourself. Our neighbor is anyone, any place in the world. This Christmas we must pray for our nation and our leaders, we must ask God to have mercy on us and to give us peace."

51

II   The Contemplatives

The Contemplatives

Many people, when they speak of contemplation, think that it means to remain silent, with your prayer almost all the time. But contemplation in the Biblical sense is not just that. "You must love God with all your heart, with all your mind and in all your activities." Well, this is contemplation. To do the will of God, with love. What makes the difference between those who love God and those who don't think of God, although they do practically the same thing with their hands, with their minds, is this: the inner quality. The inner quality is love.

FATHER RAPHAEL, *St. Andrew's Priory*

Father Timothy and Brother Dennis are so unlike each other that I wondered at first what could have brought them to the same life and into the same monastery. Timothy has the lean body of an ascetic and the gentle face of a martyr. His words flow with an easy cadence and at the end of a thought he pauses, looks at you with wet eyes, and then gently shuts them with a downward, prayerful move of his head.

Dennis is a man of work, not words. His sentences are soon outdistanced by his thoughts, his most eloquent prayers are inward and unspoken. His big hands know machines. He's a good chum.

Both men are Trappist monks. Out of a world abounding in opportunities to grasp and difficulties to surmount, journeys to undertake, babies to fondle, a world of unattainable prizes, hearty handshakes and familiar laughter, hobbies, broken hearts, choices, burdens and distractions, they have chosen to abide in silence, their lives refined to devotion. Timothy's words: "I want to love God with my whole heart, with my whole soul, with my whole being and for that I am willing to let all the things of the world go and to simplify my life so that I can gather it together into one simple act of love for God."

With Jesus Christ, and the Catholic church, I know where the truth is. I know what is interesting for me, for my salvation, for the salvation of the world, and my life is beautiful. I don't want to base my life on opinions. I would like to have certitude. A life should be based on certitude, and to me the great certitude is Jesus Christ, is the church. This is what I believe.

FATHER RAPHAEL, *St. Andrew's Priory*

Father Raphael, a Benedictine at St. Andrew's Priory in Valyermo, told me the choice of a monastic life was a simple one, no more difficult than entering engineering school or becoming a cook's apprentice. Fifty years ago in Belgium where Father Raphael professed his vows it must have been so. For Brother Dennis, the decision ripened slowly during months of prayer, months of asking and waiting for certainty. Father Timothy was a priest before he entered a monastery. He travelled occasionally on business, but his last journey was never finished. A single, swift, unreasoning detour drove him to the Abbey of Gethsemane. "The monastic vocation is part of the great mystery of Christ," he whispers, "hence the vocation itself is a great mystery."

One monastery resembles another no more, or less, than a worldly community takes after its neighbor. At the extremes are those that shun the world and others that offer it hospitality. A tiny Camaldolese hermitage overlooks the ocean from a remote headland at Big Sur. The inevitable vastness of the Pacific penetrates even the monks' tiny cells where, in isolation from his brothers, each one contemplates a private version of the mystery of Christ, performs his solitary tasks in silence, dines on austerity, and prays alone. The only voices are of gulls and waves, the only footsteps of intruders.

Other monasteries bustle — in their own quiet way. At the Benedictine monastery in Valyermo, the monks are hosts by profession. They operate a full-time retreat center. Hundreds of priests, nuns, and Catholic layworkers whose religious tasks keep them daily in the world, withdraw to Valyermo to pause in contemplation. The monks provide much more than lodging; conferences, counselling sessions, prayer meetings go on constantly. The visitors emerge recharged with new ideas and new energy. The resident monks make their own retreats at more secluded monasteries.

Of all the monasteries I visited, I became most familiar with the routine at Vina. Timothy and Dennis and their brothers are fruitgrowers. Perfect rows of walnut and plum prune trees transect the monastery lands. Some seasons are busy with harvest, others with planting or irrigation. Visitors appear rarely, and they remain

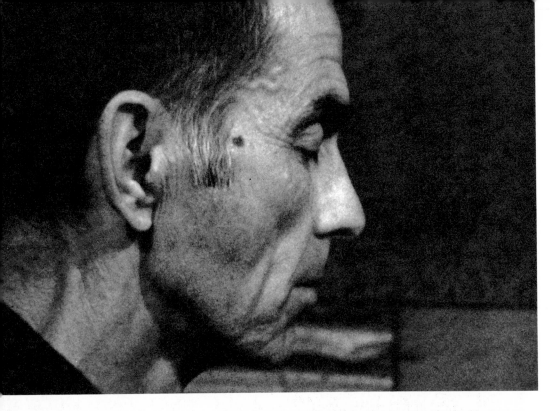

This morning, after the Divine Liturgy, I went out to the Hermitage and it was all so beautiful. The greenery of spring was coming out, the birds were singing. I went into the Hermitage and I was so aware of the presence of God. In rare moments like this I can just wrap myself in my prayer and spend as long a time as the Lord gives me grace to, just quietly being with God. Because that's what prayer really is. It's not doing something. It's just being with God, just aware of his being and forgetting all about oneself.

FATHER TIMOTHY, *Abbey of New Clairvaux*

apart from most of the community. The monk's day reflects a harmony between work and prayer, study and ritual.

3:15 A.M.	*Rise*
3:30	*Office of Vigils*
4:00–6:00	*Breakfast*
6:00	*Community Mass*
6:45–9:00	*Free Time*
9:00–12:00	*Morning work*
12:15	*Day Office*
12:30	*Lunch*
1:00–2:00	*Rest*
2:00–4:00	*Afternoon Work*
4:00–6:00	*Free Time*
6:00	*Dinner*
7:20	*Office of Vespers with Compline*
8:00 P.M.	*Retire*

During the hours of free time, Timothy withdraws to his private hermitage. Dennis takes walks in contemplation of the Lord. Some monks study, others pray, and still others serve the Lord and their brothers by working. God's will for some complements his will for others.

Words scatter thoughts, thoughts which should be gathered in God's unceasing presence. No useless word is uttered even at work or at meals. There are no idle conversations, yet friendships flourish in quiet understanding. The overwhelming impression is one of silence.

The vows of poverty, chastity, and obedience, like the daily schedule, strengthen the monk's focus on his continual and ultimate goal: the mystical knowledge of God. They are professed only after years of preparation.

Poverty is a blessing.

Celibacy weds the monk to his monastery as God made Israel his spouse. Timothy calls his life "a love affair with Christ." Just as

The most beautiful and most intense moment of prayer is when God ceases to be an object. Usually we view God as an object, we try to reach out, we put him before us, stand before him and try to grasp him as an object and we can't. He's God, he's too big; our minds are too small.

FATHER TIMOTHY, *Abbey of New Clairvaux*

At least once, sometimes twice, maybe even three times a day, I will take a walk in contemplation of the Lord because it's a tremendous opportunity to be alone with God and ponder and think of what amazing things that he has done in my life. I think about what he wants me to be, and of course, I believe that what he wants all of us to be is images of his son.

An experience of God, some kind of contact with him, leaves with it a mark on a man's soul, my soul, and it leaves a kind of impression, as if God had walked through my soul and left footprints and it's my job to fill those footprints.

I'd been in the air force three years when I realized how much more I needed to know of the Christian faith, the faith that I've held since I was a child. So I began to learn more of it and became more engrossed in it and studied it. It was a kind of thing that went along and grew like a mustard seed.

When I was young, as I was taught about the Lord Jesus, I'd always had a kind of supernatural love. I thought of him as a father or as a good man . . .

I certainly always believed he was God. As a Catholic, I had been familiar with religious orders since my youth. I realized even then that when I was around religious people or priests I felt an attraction towards that type of life.. And I felt this attraction coming back in my own life as I became more conscious of my identity as a Christian, I guess.

And so as time went on, I began to write to different orders, different houses, different monasteries, seeking information to see if that was exactly what the Lord was calling me to do because I felt the call, a vocation developing. I didn't know whether I should follow this right up as soon as I left the service, about a year away, or if I should just get a job as a mechanic.

So I decided to begin praying. And one evening as I was praying with this same question, as I got up to leave the church and was coming down the steps, it was just very clear in my mind that this was what the Lord wanted me to do immediately after discharge: to look into the religious life with the idea of entering as soon as possible.

BROTHER DENNIS, *Abbey of New Clairvaux*

a perfect human love relationship seeks a whole greater than its parts, so the monk's love finds completion in God.

Father Purcell of Mt. Calvary Episcopal monastery told me, "Obedience is intellectually the most difficult of the vows to accept, and yet the great things that have happened to me have always come through obedience."

When he is obedient to his own opinions and his own experience, even the most religious person may stray from God's plan, but the few decisions a monk makes seldom alter the course of his life and even more rarely affect the lives of others. He obeys his Abbot and shares responsibilities with his brothers. He abandons his separate identity, then resigns his personal will. He desires to will what God wills, to think with God's mind.

The monastic life is not lonely. The monk gives up the pleasures of a family and friends in return for membership in a community of brothers bound by a common purpose. He loses himself in a group of people whose well-being becomes, finally, an inseparable part of his own well-being.

"As a community, we're striving together for the monastic life of union with God. We pray and work and eat together, and we have built many of our buildings as a community. This unity of seeking the same goal by the same means, in a shared way of life — this sense of unity with my brothers is a thing that really helps my spirit. I know that this is right, that God has called these men in different times and from different parts of the world to the same place. I feel how privileged I really am to have received this call and to be able to share it with such good men as we have here in the monastery.

"I have been able to see the community as a small body of Christ, and each brother here as a different aspect of the person of Christ by the various gifts each has received from the Lord. They fit together as a unity and work as a whole by the blending of these gifts." (BROTHER DENNIS, *Vina*)

The sheer unobtrusiveness of those who have abandoned themselves to God is deceiving at first glance. When I first met the Carmelite sisters of Reno, they seemed so plain, so ordinary, so wholly lacking in definition that I was aware of nothing special about them except a great feeling of ease and comfort in their company. Only gradually did I perceive their spiritual radiance. Later I was haunted by the memory of their simplicity and grace.

At first the contemplative life appeared to me a unilateral affair, a one-way street of monks offering themselves to God. Then I sensed that something else was there. One day I went up to the Abbot at the Vina monastery and told him I felt that the monks receive something from God in return. The abbot beamed, delighted that I had seen this. I received the same delighted reaction from other monks, but initially they were shy in discussing it and too humble to suggest that their devotion was so generously rewarded. The grace of God is something the outsider may not feel or even believe, but I have no doubt that it is the keystone of the monastic experience.

"I gradually became aware of grace because it's not just any joy, it's the joy of the Holy Spirit, it's the joy in spiritual realities. It's not any peace, it's the peace that Jesus brings, it's the peace the world tries to give but doesn't seem to be able to. It's the peace in knowing that you are secure. I like to think of it as going upstream to the source of this grace, where our destiny lies." (BROTHER DENNIS, *Vina*)

Timothy and Dennis live in a way which invites the grace of God. That is the simple purpose of monasticism. But the total quality of the monastic experience is impossible to communicate, impossible even for a frequent visitor to grasp. Ideas like community brotherhood, spiritual marriage, and intimate union with God continually grow in meaning when they are the substances of life for decades, for a lifetime. In the end, to seek God means to welcome God, not to look for him but to recognize his presence and receive his grace. Brother Dennis explained:

"As I have spent more and more time in the monastery, it has become increasingly clear to me that what the Lord is asking me is not so much what I can do, not so much what I can act like or try to improve, but just simply to be there, to be available to God, to be present to him and to be at peace in his presence."

III   Two Old World Traditions

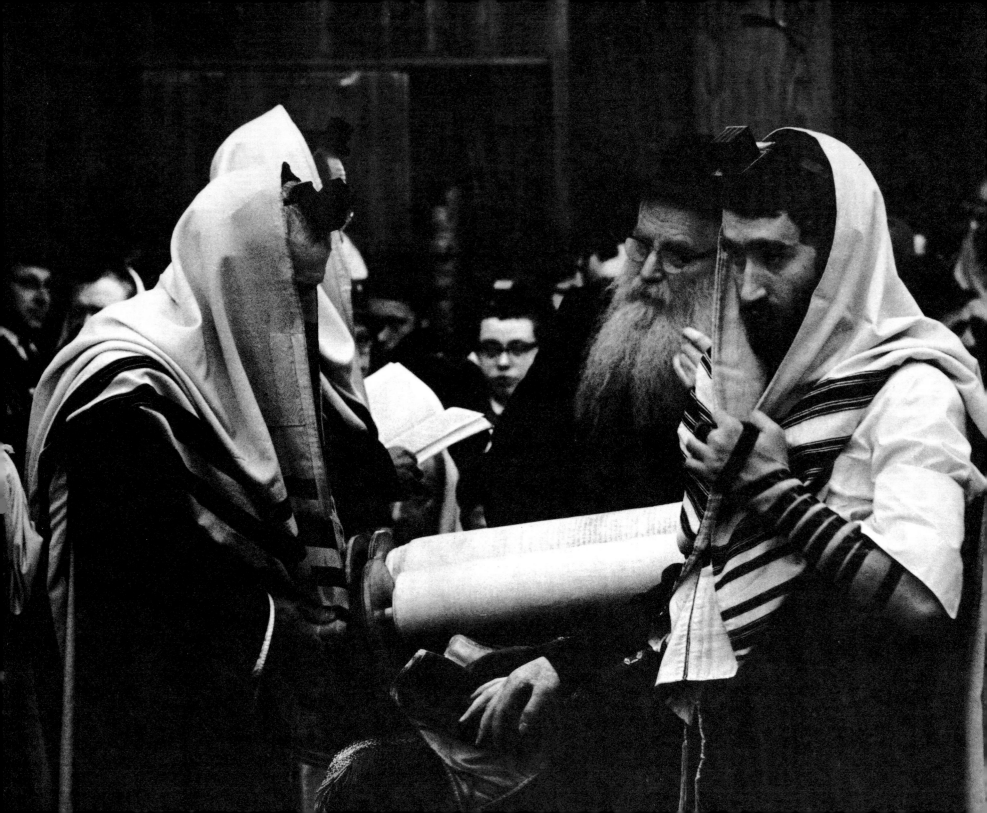

The Hasidim

I wonder if the Hasidic Jew lies motionless when he sleeps? All the rest of his life is blurred by movement.

His feet stamp the sidewalk as he hurries to the synagogue or rise in bold steps in a traditional wedding dance.

Stroking his long beard, twisting his sidelocks, gesturing vehemently in discussion, his hands never nap curled up in a pocket. They monopolize his conversations.

In prayer, he rocks. Back and forth, back and forth his prayer shawl flutters. Its fringes quiver. Is the prayer, too, a dance? Does he rock to its music or is he carried away to the mystical heart of Hasidism?

The motion, the dancing began in the mid-seventeen hundreds when simple people whose souls hungered for God watched the Baal Shem Tov, founder of Hasidism and subject of legend, as he prayed. He moved. He had rhythm, song, concentration, intensity. He felt joy. What they saw was ecstasy — a gift to the broken-spirited Judaism of that time.

Hasidism flourished in Eastern Europe until the early twentieth century. The humble and the devoted held fast to it in Cossack haunted villages called "shtetls." In each one a different rebbe, a "proven one" of God, gathered his court of disciples tightly around him. Then, as its leadership lost inspiration, the music of Hasidism began to fade. The Nazi holocaust nearly silenced it.

Some rebbes who survived, or their descendants, moved with their followers to the U.S. and settled in Brooklyn, N.Y. Other Jews like Leibel Bistritsky, subject of the film *Lubavitch,* joined them, and the new Hasidic communities swelled in size. Today there are about a dozen different groups in Brooklyn. The Lubavitcher is one of the largest. The Hasidic population in the U.S. is difficult to estimate, but it probably numbers between 20,000 and 40,000 people.

The Hasidim are more than extremely devout Jews. In fact, Orthodox Jews do not regard them as the custodians of true Judaism. The Hasidim have enriched the basic tradition with a mystical dimension and, with the rebbe at the center, have wrapped the swaddling of religion around and around each of their communities.

Like Orthodox Judaism, the practice of Hasidism begins and ends with the law of God. The Torah (the first five books of the

Old Testament) sets forth the law, the other Scriptures amplify it. Centuries of changing historical circumstances have refracted it into myriad subtleties, explicated in volumes of rabbinical works, which anticipate and prescribe behavior for even the most obscure human event. Every human action is thus a collaboration with the divine because each is performed in obedience or disobedience of God.

The Hasid perceives that righteousness requires more than living the law, that it is a collaboration with his fellow men. He knows that no single prayer ascends alone to God without bearing witness to the prayers of all. In every aspect of his life and toward all members of creation, he exhibits the love which he feels for God.

The synagogue is the center of his life and the center of the community. Homely and unembellished both inside and out, it is a place to meet not only to pray and to celebrate, but to argue with energetic devotion the subtle intricacies of Torah. The synagogue is the place where one sees and hears the Rebbe, the unifying spirit of the community.

It is impossible to exaggerate the importance of the Rebbe to a Hasidic Jew. He is a "wonder man" capable of extraordinary feats of wisdom. He is a source of guidance at every threshold of his followers' lives. He approves their marriages, advises them on business ventures or travel, sorts out family problems, inspires the discouraged, and intercedes on behalf of the needy. Members of the Lubavitch community may see the Rebbe daily, yet still they stand eagerly at his doorway hoping for another glimpse of his face. The same followers, when they hear him speak, gather every one of his words into their memories to keep and to ponder. They cherish most of all the few private meetings they have with him each year.

"The first time I saw the Lubavitcher Rebbe he impressed me very deeply," said Leibel Bistritsky, speaking with that eloquent formality so characteristic of many Hasidic Jews, "and with his beautiful eyes he penetrated me so that I became one of his disciples just by feeling, by emotion. He is my leader spiritually and also physically. He shows me how to go in the straight, righteous way. He arouses in me the desire and the understanding how to keep the Torah. He exemplifies to me how I should pray, how I should

behave. Because he understands better than I what is the correct way in life."

The Rebbe is one who sees more clearly the true, perfectly integrated nature of God. For love of his brothers, out of compassion for their earthbound souls and for the shattered divinity of all creation, he struggles to lead them from the multiplicity of earthly experience toward that unified vision of God which is obscured by the cloud of man's imperfections.

The Hasidic mystic seeks not an arcane but a pure knowledge of God. He attempts to reconcile the divinity which dwells within all matter, that which is of the substance of God, with the totality of God which is remote and elusive. Because God is partially disclosed in nature, the Hasid interacts with him and works toward separating good from evil, releasing the divine sparks which are imprisoned in materality and bringing ever nearer the moment when the world is restored to perfection. Hasidism proclaims that each unique being exists for the purpose of advancing the ultimate salvation of all creation.

The Hasid fears God as a man fears the power of his beloved, trembling for her nearness while dreading her disfavor. He loves and fears, feels fascination and awe. The rapture of knowing and longing to know more of God is evident in the passion with which the Hasidim pray, dance, sing, and argue, in the whole-hearted gladness with which they live.

Children, many of them, are the greatest of earthly joys. To the Hasid, they are a manifestation of his own life. They carry him forward in time. He loves to hear their noisiness, to share their vivacity. I've been to several "farbrengen," or gatherings, where the children were playing so loudly that you could barely hear the revered Rebbe speak, yet no one rebuked them.

"Everyone wants to have a child. When you're young you always want to have, first, a boy, because if you have a boy then you can have a bris, a circumcision." So said Leibel Bistritsky on the eve of the circumcision of his grandson.

The next day dozens of friends and relatives filled Leibel's apartment in Brooklyn. His son, struggling to contain his excite-

Every fall comes that time in the Jewish calendar
known as the Days of Awe. "During this month we
have the most important holidays of the year," explains
Bistritsky. "One is the New Year, Rosh Hashanah, when
a person prays for the well-being of his family. For
eight days afterward a person repents his misdeeds
toward almighty God. The end of the repentance days is
called Yom Kippur, the highest day of the Jewish
religion when the person fasts for 24 hours and prays
to God for forgiveness." Every Hasid performs
a ritual known as "shlug kapporus". Swinging a live
chicken in a circle above his head, he transfers his sins
to it by prayer, then has the fowl slaughtered in
atonement.

73

In preparation for the festival of Passover, all foods that contain "hametz" (leavening) must be removed from the house and burned. During the festival unleavened Passover bread, "matzot," is eaten with bitter herbs to commemorate the hasty meal consumed by the children of Israel as they fled Egypt.

The Feast of Purim, described in the Biblical Book of Esther, celebrates the Jews' victory over their would-be exterminators in the time of the Persian king, Ahasuerus. Gifts of delicacies are shared with friends; alms are given to the poor. Children dress in costumes and beg door to door:

Heintz iz Purim, morgen iz aus
Gib mir a dreier, und warft mich araus.

(Purim lasts only a day at a time,
Throw me out, but spare me a dime.)

It is said of the harvest festival of "Succot": "Ye shall take you, on the first day, the fruit of a goodly tree, palm branches, foliage of leafy trees, and willows of the brook, and ye shall rejoice before the Lord your God." (LEV. 23:40) Succot begins four days after Yom Kippur. Strictly observant Jews pray with imported "lulav" (palm fronds) and "etrog" (fragrant citron).

76

ment and pride, explained, "This is what any religious man looks forward to . . . is making a bris. It's a son to carry on your name, to carry on your part of your religion."

The unknowing infant, meanwhile, is in capable hands. The special Rabbi who performs the circumcision is a master of the technique. His reputation is built on the speed and smoothness with which he carries out the operation.

The next major event in the youth's life is his bar mitzvah, the beginning of a Jew's manhood. Among Hasidim the bar mitzvah receives less celebration and ritual than in Orthodox or Conservative Judaism. More important is the training which precedes it.

"Every person wants his children to go in his footsteps," says Bistritsky, "and he wants his children to learn the Torah, to go according to Jewish law. He wants them to understand and to feel the same way he feels. That is the reason why we send our children to the Yeshiva [school] so they get the right education according to the Torah and what the Torah demands from us."

Hasidic children spend up to ten hours a day at school. All morning they study Torah, all afternoon the required public school curriculum. The classes are far livelier than any I remember having. Often the teacher presents a puzzle, some life situation, and asks how the Scriptures require it to be solved. Hands leap up and voices stutter in eagerness to provide the answer. The miniature, beardless Hasids argue fine points of Scripture with all the vehemence of their elders.

Lubavitch teaching includes the Tanya and the Gemara. A young teenager told me, "Tanya explains about the soul, that you have two parts of you. You have a good part and the bad part. It tells how one is going against the other trying to win over the person and explains how you should try to become better, how to defeat the bad one and become completely good. Gemara is the law. Everybody has to live by this. You see, if you don't know about the soul, then you still can follow the laws of the Gemara. If there is a situation and you need to know what you should do, so you look in the Gemara and you find out. But the Tanya is the meaning of everything, why you do this, and how it connects you to God."

The Hasidic youth knows the priorities. Another explained,

"Fun we have after school and after our homework is done . . . then we run around a little for our health, so the next day we'll be able to come to school and learn better, feeling refreshed."

After the equivalent of high-school graduation, the Hasid proceeds to unravel more intricate Judaic texts, working by himself or in collaboration with other students. His study is comparable to seminary training. The supervision is minimal but the learning is intensive, the hours endless. From the age of seventeen or eighteen to about twenty-three, young Hasidim spend almost every moment of the day at the Yeshiva or in the synagogue nearby.

When his formal education is complete he may be ordained as a Rabbi. Nearly all male Hasidim achieve this level of education, although only some become Rabbis.

Just before his ordination, Leibel Bistritsky's family decided he should go into business. Naturally he obeyed and now he runs a Kosher delicatessen on Manhattan's lower East Side. Every afternoon other devout Jews gather in his store for the Minhah prayer.

No matter what his business, the Hasid tries to live and work as near to his synagogue as possible, to be as much with other Hasidim as he can, and to keep a schedule which allows him time for the daily prayers and days off for the holidays. If he must choose between a poor job and a good one which interferes with his worship, the decision is easy.

As soon as he finishes his studies, a young Hasid gets married. An unmarried Hasid is an unfinished adult.

For the Hasidic woman, marriage and motherhood are the highest goals in life, the only ones open to her of any importance. Women play no part in religious ceremonies, have no leadership expectations in the community, rarely have jobs, and have little authority even in their own homes. Their religious education is distinctly different from that of men. Their purpose is to produce and raise proper Jewish children.

Marriages are arranged by matchmakers. "Obviously it's not done by ourselves, the whole day we are in Yeshiva," said Eli Bornstein, a Lubavitcher, shortly before his wedding. "It's arranged by close friends of the family or through members of the family who

Because Hasidic interpretation of Torah forbids a man to put a blade to his face, Hasidic boys wear sidelocks and adult men have full beards. Other laws require men to keep their heads covered at all times in respect to God, hence the characteristic hat or yarmulke.

When a person gets married the whole idea is that this woman becomes his wife and she is not allowed to anybody else. Marriage brings two people together and separates the woman from the rest of the world. So at the marriage reception the men and women are kept separate.

ELI BORNSTEIN

happen to know the other side."

Once the matchmaker has brought two people together, it takes little time for a wedding to be announced.

"I met her several times, about six or seven times, and we discussed different topics. I went to her house and then we went to see different sights of New York City together, took the Circle Line tour. Then we figured that was enough and we decided to become engaged."

Marriage raises a man to a higher spiritual level. Its awesome importance and weighty responsibilities are impressed upon the groom as he hears his marriage contract read before an assembly of male relatives and friends.

The wedding takes place outdoors that the fruit of it might multiply like the stars of the sky. As the ceremony begins, Eli Bornstein meets his bride under the "hupeh," the wedding canopy. Her face is veiled. His, unshielded, is lustrously pale. His eyes glisten, his breathing is imperceptible. Relatives pressed close to the couple seem literally to hold them up.

With a swiftness that husband and wife will disbelieve ever after, the blessings are pronounced, Eli shatters the ritual glass underfoot, and the bride's veil is lifted. Instantly a grin of utter relief and joy transforms the groom's face, and with a burst of music the ecstatic celebration begins.

Once married, the Hasid begins a life which varies little from year to year. He continues to study Biblical texts, he prays with increasing devotion, he looks forward with eagerness to audiences with his Rebbe, and he works hard to support a growing family.

One of the constants is the daily prayer with Tfillin (or phylacteries), considered supremely important by the Lubavitcher Hasidim. According to Lubavitch interpretation of Talmud, the door of the future world is completely locked to the Jew who has not at least once in his life put on the Tfillin. As Bistritsky explained: "When a Jew gets up in the morning one of the first things he does is to say his morning prayers. Every morning except Saturdays and holidays he first puts on Tfillin. Tfillin consists of two specially prepared leather boxes containing certain Biblical scriptures. One

of these is bound on the upper arm opposite the heart, the other is placed on the head. This very important observance signifies the submission of the heart and mind to God."

The Lubavitchers have a widespread Tfillin campaign. They travel around in a kind of temple on wheels, stopping at street corners and asking Jews if they have put on Tfillin that day. If a Jew admits he hasn't, they beckon him inside, adjust the phylacteries on his arm and head, and begin the prayers.

One time when I was flying from New York to Los Angeles I noticed on the plane with me an old Lubavitcher Hasid whom I had met some years earlier. As I expected, he made his way from his seat to mine with Tfillin in hand. He asked me if I had put on Tfillin that day (my answer was no) and proceeded to help me off with my jacket, roll up my sleeve, crown me with a hat, and put on the Tfillin. Right there in the airplane.

In this and other ways the Lubavitchers have a worldwide campaign to remind the Jewish population of its rich traditions and to lift up their souls toward God. They operate dozens of schools and centers around the United States and in other countries and recently they have opened "Habad Houses" on college campuses where students may discover what Bistritsky calls "the happiness and joy of how a Jew lives."

The Hasid has no need for television, movies, or parties. Such amusements are literally diversions which would only distract him from his soul's object and seem frivolous by comparison.

What the Hasidim delight in, especially the Lubavitcher, is the farbrengen, the gathering at which the Rebbe addresses his followers. Farbrengens take place after the principal festivals of the Jewish calendar and at the end of certain Hasidic holidays.

Eager Hasidim fill the synagogue hours before the farbrengen is to start. Later arrivals jostle the early ones to get places near the table where the Rebbe will sit. Soon the jostling turns to pushing and the pushing to shoving as more and more people squeeze into the hall long after it seems possible to wedge in one more human being.

Elbows of tall men box the ears of youths. The room becomes

*In order to explain to you the connection between the
soul and almighty God, I will give you an example of
a rope. When the soul comes down it is connected to
almighty God with a full rope, a rope made up of many
strands. If you live a life as a good Jew and if you live
a life according to the law, then this rope is never cut
off. If, God forbid, you do something which is not
according to the law one of the strands is ripped. A
person has only so many strands until he loses his
connection. I don't think there is a human being who
can say that by him never a strand was broken.*

*A Hasid repents not only because he fears the punish-
ment from God, but also because he loves God so much
and he loves the law of God and the ways of God so
much that he then gets a different kind of fear — a
fear of the greatness of God.*

LEIBEL BISTRITSKY

*If you live in a Hasidic atmosphere and you're around
these people, you can't forget. Even if you don't look
at the book, you can't go off. You go to synagogue.
You're with ultra-religious, ultra-orthodox people.
You live with the people like you see around my father's
house. All religious children. Every boy wearing a
yarmulke, every boy and girl going to Yeshiva. And I
feel that I will raise my children the same way I was
raised.*

LEIBEL BISTRITSKY'S SON

dense with black-suited bodies. Dizzying, faceless rows of identical black hats and thick eyeglasses climb in tiers almost to the ceiling, as if a tower of holy men were ascending toward Heaven itself. The devoted stand on tiptoe and tilt forward dangerously in frantic anticipation, hushing each other into silence, as the Rebbe enters. At 8:30 the farbrengen begins. Some last until four in the morning.

The Rebbe addresses the crowd in half-hour segments. He discusses community policy and interprets passages of Scripture, tells stories and glorifies the law. His words have the rhythm of prayer.

Between one topic and another he rocks, a Hasidic melody springs to his lips, and the entire assembly echoes his song. Shoulder pressed to shoulder, the enormous mass of swaying Hasidim dance themselves weary as a single black body.

"Sometimes you hear the Rebbe cry, and once you hear him cry, you yourself feel like crying," Bistritsky recalled. "It has an effect on you. Or you see that he's happier, so you yourself feel a little happier. The person who leads you, he has the effect on you spiritually."

The spellbinder grasps the souls of his followers, and with words like the wheels of the Baal-Shem's famous coach he transports them through time and space, and enfeebles history. Conjuring the scents of rich ointments and moist gardens, he breaks their hearts with scattered Israel's longing and heals them with the joy of a king's son restored to his throne. Then in silence the Rebbe departs.

Exhausted and exalted by singing and dancing, dazed with rapture, the Hasid stumbles home to his bed and, at last, to the stillness of sleep. But in his dreams, surely his soul must dance. Bistritsky echoed the Baal-Shem's message:

"There is nothing in this world, no movement of a hand, no movement of the human person which is not controlled by God. If a leaf falls down from a tree and turns in certain directions and flies one way and another, it has to do with a connection with almighty God.

"Every soul which a Jew has in himself is a spark of almighty God. This spark livens him. It was sent down to accomplish a mission in life and afterwards this spark is returned to almighty God."

Hasidut tells you the deeper things in life. It tells you the emotional and spiritual way to live as a Jew.

LEIBEL BISTRITSKY

The Hutterites

I posed what I thought was a simple question: "Would you rather drive a tractor in the field or work the cattle on the range?"

Any farm boy could have readily made a choice, but the young Hutterite I asked was frankly perplexed by the question. Nothing in his upbringing had prepared him to consider work as a matter of personal preference. At the age of fifteen he is assigned a task, and whatever it is he does it.

Very few indeed are the personal decisions a Hutterite makes in his life. He chooses to be baptized into the Hutterite church. He selects a wife. All of his other decisions are either trivial or vitally connected to the welfare of his community.

The Hutterites live frugally, sharing in common all things material and spiritual. They are pacifists, not utopians. Their goal has never been to establish a perfect society, although they haven't the slightest doubt that theirs is superior to "wordly" societies. They simply live the way God obliges man to live, as they interpret the gospels, because it is the safest and surest way to be rescued from sin.

The Hutterites recognize but one true church, the apostolic community founded on the day of Pentecost by the Holy Spirit. True believers in Christ must enter this church voluntarily, by baptism, and follow its rules:

"The whole group of believers was united heart and soul; no one claimed for his own use anything he had, as everything they owned was held in common. . . . None of their members was ever in want, as all those who owned land or houses would sell them, and bring the money from them, to present it to the apostles; it was then distributed to any members who might be in need." (Acts 4:32–34)

"You must love not this passing world . . . nothing this world has to offer—the sensual body, the lustful eye, pride in possessions —could ever come from the Father but only from the world. And the world, with all it craves for, is coming to an end; but anyone who does the will of God remains for ever." (I John 2:15–17)

". . . it is a narrow gate and a hard road that leads to life, and only a few find it." (Matt. 7:14)

The first Hutterite community was founded in Moravia in 1528 by a group of refugee Anabaptists. (Hutterian historiographers say the true church was "restored" in this year.) Because they rejected infant baptism and insisted on total separation of church and state, these religious nonconformists, historical and spiritual cousins of the Old Order Amish and the Mennonites, were continual victims of persecution during the chaotic years of collapsing feudal society and sectarian turmoil that accompanied the Reformation.

Persecutions hounded the Hutterites from Moravia to Hungary and on to the Ukraine. Opposition to Russian military induction forced them, between 1874 and 1877, to migrate to North America. Their conscientious objection to military service, resistance to integration into public school systems, and prodigious land buying have made difficulties for the Hutterites in the United States, but nevertheless they have prospered. The original 800 immigrants in three colonies in South Dakota have grown to over 22,000 in 229 colonies in the United States and Canada. Most colonies own between three and seven thousand acres of land.

I asked an older man, "What does it mean to be a Hutterite?"

"It means a great life," he responded. "It means living in a community where I can seek salvation. It's living up to the Word of God."

The Hutterites expect the worst from the world outside their colonies and are never pleasantly surprised. Their pessimism arises not only from a history of persecution, but also from a world view which considers all men to be born in sin, inclined to evil, and restored to holiness only by a repentant death.

"We believe the Lord does not want us to be condemned to Hell, so we try to save one another from sin and try to do as much good to our fellow men as possible. We believe that every living soul can be saved from condemnation."

"Ordnung regiert die Welt," say the Hutterites: "Order rules the world." In their four-hundred year history, they have raised to a divine principle the motto: "A place for everything and everything in its place." Events in a Hutterite community are no more random than the celestial activities of stars and planets.

The colony bell tolls the rising time; it calls the people to meals and it sends them out to work. The community decides not only what its members should do, but also when they should do it.

If the fifteen-year-old gets to drive one of the big tractors, a field boss will tell him what to do. If he's assigned to the pigs, the pig boss makes sure the pens are clean and the shoats are fed. The bosses take orders from the manager of the colony. The manager obeys the preacher and the preacher, who is chosen by lot from a number of candidates by a council of elders, relies on written tradition and group consensus to make his decisions.

The will of the community and the harmony of its members express the supreme authority of God on earth. Each person knows his place: parents discipline children, older dominates younger, men rule women, blood relations are loyal to each other. Only by surrendering to the will of the group, by receiving discipline from those above him and by rendering it to those below, can an individual sidestep the pitfalls of sin and qualify for a place in Heaven.

Hutterite discipline in practice is not nearly so dull, repressive, or gloomy as it sounds. The elders know not only the rules, they know human nature as well. How can a boy settle down to work if he doesn't sneak into town to satisfy his curiosity? If a girl paints her toenails with glossy red polish and hides the secret pleasure inside her stout black boots, well, such vanity will pass. Hutterites know that all men are sinners and that children, especially, can't help being willful. They never punish a child because he is "bad." (No one is completely "good," after all.) They invariably link the punishment to an undesirable behavior. Their goal is a well-behaved child, not a guilty one.

Life in the colonies I visited seemed so peaceful and satisfying, and above all so consummately sane, that I almost regret I was not born into one. A few outsiders have attempted to join the Hutterites, but the elders have discouraged them because they know that by the time one reaches adulthood it is far too late. Respect for authority, loyalty to the group, passivity, and sharing are traits rewarded by the Hutterites from infancy. Individual success, innovation for its own sake, competitiveness, and "self-discipline" are cleanly and efficiently rubbed out by a process of gentle persuasion called (misleadingly) "breaking the child's will."

David Waldner is a handsome example of this upbringing, and it's no surprise that he is a teacher and manager of the Rosedale Colony in South Dakota. He stands out in my memory as a model of faith, one of the few real "heroes" I've run into in my life. No doubt he views himself very differently, if he thinks about himself at all.

David is the first Hutterite I met. He was leading a pied-piperish band of frolicking children toward one of the barns when I drove up the rutted colony driveway raising a long cloud of dust. A dozen mild faces crowned with black hats or covered with dotted kerchiefs turned and scrutinized us as the cloud settled around my car. Gazing at us, Waldner seemed a tall, raven-suited, bushy-bearded statue of suspicion and condemnation. I felt a twinge of embarrassment for the sinful world I represented as this stern, upright man examined me.

Children are our foundation. If they aren't brought up right, if they aren't taught right, it's a great hindrance. It's a liability.

JOSHUA WOLLMAN

But I misread him. His stiffness was only Hutterite caution and reserve. He greeted me kindly in the thick German accent of his Tyrolean ancestors.

"Well, come up to the house," he said. "You'll have something to eat."

All his invitations were made in the imperative: "Put your jacket here; wash up there; now, sit down in this place and eat this sandwich. We'll walk around the colony after we eat . . ." It was understood: I was the guest, he was the "host." Naturally he knew what was best for me.

As we toured the colony, David answered even my naivest questions directly and without hesitation. He never made me feel foolish for knowing little about turkeys or, worse yet, Hutterian Christianity. David never equivocated. "Well, I just don't know," he would confess when I asked him a stumper. He taught me how easy it is for a strong, confident person to recognize and accept the boundaries of his ignorance.

We inspected dairy cows and sheep, truck gardens, wheat fields, and sheds of gleaming tractors and harvesting combines. Straight lines connect all points. So orderly and fixed are the design of Hutterite colonies that a member of one colony could automatically find his way at another. The buildings smite you with their aluminum-sided ugliness and clash with the archaic costumes of the people. The Hutterites have decided that where it profits the colony without threatening moral disruption or benefitting the members unequally, modern technology is acceptable. Indeed, it is necessary.

How else to support the colony's skyrocketing population and still lay aside capital for expansion? When a colony gets crowded, when having too many hands and too little work invites the temptations of idleness, the elders look for land — sometimes far across the state if the price is right. Lots are cast, and half the families of of the old colony move to the new one. Seventy-five to one hundred fifty persons live in most colonies.

Whenever I paused in my questions, David asked me a few of his own. He was very curious about me, about my work, the way I lived, the places I'd visited, but his wasn't the curiosity of one who

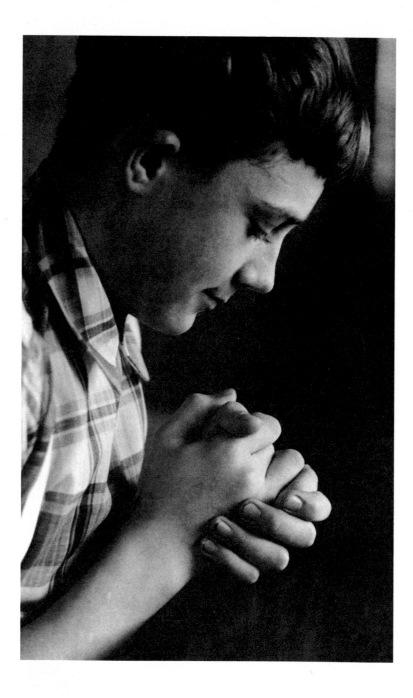

has been deprived of a chance to see the world. He made me feel that it was me he wanted to know about, that my experience was important to him.

There must be more than a dozen men named David Waldner in the Hutterite population. The Hutterites have very few family names among them and are sparing with given names as well. Often all the youngsters of one colony are first cousins and are forbidden by convention to "date" each other. Visits to other colonies are opportunities to find sweethearts. The girls put on their most flamboyantly printed muslins; the boys may sneak in a contraband transistor radio. Teenagers are always the most eager members of the harvesting details and round-up gangs that travel to neighboring colonies.

A couple who "go together" are in for plenty of teasing from younger brothers and sisters, and many understandings are kept happily secret. Courtship often lasts for several years and marriage never takes place until both parties are baptized, usually after the age of twenty. Invariably the bride moves to her husband's colony. A man does not become a voting member of the colony until he is both baptized and married.

David's family inhabits a blindingly spotless, unadorned apartment in one of the graceless residence buildings. The eyes of a guest wander uselessly in search of some peculiarity of design or embellishment, an object out of place, a blemish on the linoleum floor. Mrs. Waldner does her spring cleaning every week. No frivolous decoration, no graven image violates the splendid bareness of her well-scrubbed walls.

The Hutterites enjoy none of the world's entertainments. "What do you look forward to all day?" I asked a man at Poinsett colony.

"Well, I enjoy most of all passing the evening with my family," answered the father of eight, "teaching them the ways of the Lord."

David and his family, like everyone else, eat all their meals in the big communal dining hall which they call the "kitchen." It is more than an eating place. The kitchen is the geographical and social center of the community. I worried about and finally asked,

It is our custom not to decorate our houses a great deal and not to take too much pride in things that are man-made.

JOSHUA WOLLMAN

"What if you get hungry between meals?" David assured me that was no problem. Each person or family receives "snacks" to take home. They also get a monthly allowance of wine.

Food is much more than mere nourishment for the Hutterites. In fact, food and prayer are so intimately joined that a Hutterite automatically folds his hands in the proper manner no matter where he eats, even in a roadside cafe. A newborn baby hears a prayer before and after he nurses. Children are never disciplined by depriving them of food, but one of the worst punishments is to be ostracized at mealtimes.

The Hutterites enjoy the freshest of home-grown meats and vegetables. Out of their kitchens come crusty loaves of pumpernickel, thick fruity jams and preserves, spring lamb, old-fashioned pork sausages, dumplings, light prairie honey. When the moment of eating arrives, in between the first grace and the last grace, the banquet vanishes with astonishing speed. No talking is allowed at meals and I doubt that anyone would have time for it. Only a few playful children or conspiring adolescents even look up from their plates or glance across the room at the tables of the opposite sex.

When the preacher leaves his apartment every evening for the community prayers, his wife and children, in order of age, follow like ducklings behind him. As he passes each family's apartment, the people fall into step behind him and march in procession to the schoolhouse, where the men and women separate and enter by different doors. Everyone knows exactly where to sit according to age and sex. They spend half an hour at prayer.

Sunday mornings the service lasts an hour and a half. Flanked by the elders of the community, the preacher admonishes his stern-faced brothers and sisters from behind the teacher's worn old desk. The smooth surface of the blackboard behind him has been washed clean; bits of chalk rest in formation on its sill. It is the spirit of the service, not its locale, that is sacred. Wherever there is order is the domain of God.

The preacher reads ponderously from seventeenth-century Hutterite texts, chanting the formal High German sentences in a peculiar liturgical cadence. (No preacher would indulge himself or expose others to error by authoring his own sermon.) The congregation sings responsively as he leads them in a traditional hymn. Many of these extraordinary anthems were written in foul dungeons by sixteenth-century Hutterites in anticipation of martyrdom. The words exhort the brethren to persevere in spite of their tribulations in this transitory world. Women's voices compete with the monotonous basses and baritones, loudly claiming their only opportunity to dominate, as the hymn is offered to God without thought of beauty or "carnal joy." A soft prayer and benediction conclude the service.

Life in the colonies never impressed me as manifestly "religious." There are no private mystics there. No inspired individuals dazzle their fellows with startling interpretations of the word of God. But Hutterites don't forget for an instant why they live differently from other people, why they hold all goods in common, disdain wordly vanities, deplore idleness, and confess their sins. From birth until death, every deed and every thought is a preparation for the kingdom of Heaven.

Men like David Waldner understand their place in life and have no reason to fear death. They know how to relate to the earth, to animals, to other human beings. All these things are clear to them because they understand their own relationship to God.

It happened that a well-known elder of a neighboring colony died while I was at Rosedale and I attended his funeral. Hundreds of oldtimers and their families came from colonies as distant as Canada to honor the deceased. Grieved, self-contained men dressed in new black clothing filled one half of the colony's big dining hall. Sobbing women crowded the other half as young men of the dead one's family inched into the room, straining under an enormous coffin. In life, someone whispered to me, the dead man weighed 300 lbs.

Dry, lifeless prairie air seeping through the windows did nothing to relieve the stagnant heat as the colony preacher read monotonously in German. Men and women listened impassively, hands folded in their laps. The sermon lasted over an hour.

When it ended the mourners followed the plain, wooden

coffin, now nailed shut, to the hill-top burial ground. Their numbers blackened the parched green slope. The coffin thudded unceremoniously into its dry grave and a dozen fast-working young men flung the dirt in after it. When the hole was filled and the gray earth tamped with the back of a shovel, the bereaved Hutterites turned their backs on the grave and walked away.

There was a generous dinner for the visitors that night and a rare bottle of beer. The mood was not quite festive, but sorrow seemed to give way to gladness that another soul was at last at rest. The old man had died slowly, with many long nights to remember and confess every one of his sins. He was ready for salvation.

In the old days, an elder told me, they simply wrapped a dead person in a bag, dropped him in a hole, and covered it up. That was all. There is no need to elaborate on death. All of life is an anticipation of this passing over.

Hutterites warn misbehaving children: "Be good or we'll let a *Draussiger* [outsider] take you!" The threat is effective. Life in the world is unknown and unpredictable; that of the colony certain and orderly. Outside, men do violence to each other; within, rarely is a single word uttered in anger. Centuries-old texts and unwritten conventions anticipate and deter nearly all possible conflicts. Each member knows exactly what the rules are and what every situation demands of him.

Those of us who live in the world might examine our notion of the word "freedom" and consider the time and effort we are obliged to spend choosing one path or another, "improving" ourselves, competing, hurting others, making millions of trivial decisions, worrying, or dreaming. "In a Hutterite colony, a man is free of many pressures except as he brings them upon himself," writes a Hutterite preacher. "He has much time to think and reflect." There are some who equate freedom with the opportunity to make mistakes. For the Hutterite, the only freedom worth pursuing is freedom from sin. But on a milk-warm summer evening, as he rests with others on the lawn outside the dining hall and listens to games played by tireless children, perhaps he reflects with pleasure on the burdens that are not his.

IV   In Search of Alternatives

Reba Place Fellowship

One of the important things about life in the Fellow-ship is that the problems get solved. People change. In my experience, most people don't change very much. Their problems just persist year after year. It's really very gratifying to be here where people are changing before your eyes.

JEANNE

"If you have the notion that people who live in a religiously centered community like Reba Place Fellowship are very spiritual and just don't have human problems any more," Jeanne told me, "you are badly mistaken. That's not the case at all. We live together in a very human way. We believe it's vital to be who we are with each other, to be honest and get things out in the open, and then to discover areas where healing needs to take place. It's just anything but ideal, it's anything but beautiful and noble. It's very nitty-gritty and very real."

Jeanne and her husband Alan are the heads of one of the families of Christians who live on a street called Reba Place in Evanston, Illinois. The household includes their three children; Hilda, a single woman who, like Alan, is an elder of the Fellowship; David and Robin, a young married couple; Melene and her daughter; and five other young men and women. Their house bulges with porches and gables. They call it Toad Hall.

The God who is worshipped at Toad Hall is as real and nitty-gritty as the crayon marks scribbled up and down the wall next to the stairway, as inescapable as the clatter and soot of the nearby elevated railroad, and as palpable as the soap suds and dinner

Before I got into this life in Christian community, I defined myself by my job; I was what I did. And what I did was teach high school English — I gave myself wholly to that job. I had all the limitations that one can have in that profession: Life turned on having commas in the right place, nothing was as exciting as reading Shakespeare, and I was very disappointed when other people didn't agree with that. I was closed off, uptight, caught by fears. I didn't understand myself at all; I could be swept about by whatever influence came along. It was then that I started to pray. Now I know that I need Jesus and I need to be a Christian. That has drawn my whole life together and given it meaning.

The life at Reba is a total life. When people used to visit me here, they'd ask, "Do you get down to the Loop for cultural events?" and I used to say proudly, "Yes, indeed. We go down to the Symphony." I wanted them to know that we weren't behind in any way. But now, while it is true that some people do go out, I no longer feel defensive about being consumed by the Fellowship. If there is time for something extra, fine, but so often things come up that require your attention, you just give up those little plans to go off by yourself. It's a total commitment.

JEANNE

dishes in the kitchen sink. He is equally familiar. To him and his works they attribute no special elegance; he participates in everything mundane. He honors prayers for assistance in obtaining a driver's license ("Please don't let me forget my turn signals . . .") or for relieving a nasty headache with the same benevolence as requests for endurance and faith. "He has his own personal flair," David commented familiarly.

Not all of the one hundred adults and sixty children of Reba Place Fellowship are members of households like the one at Toad Hall. Nuclear families and single individuals who belong to the Fellowship live in houses and apartments nearby. They call themselves members of Christ's body and Reba Place Fellowship a "living church."

The Fellowship began seventeen years ago with one single goal: to put the word of the gospels into practice in daily life. Inspired by the radical Christianity of sixteenth- and seventeenth-century Anabaptism, the Christians of Reba Place repeated the effort made by Hutterites, Mennonites, and Amish four centuries ago to reconstruct the apostolic church of Jerusalem in a "modern" world.

Because this world is so vastly unlike the one in which the Hutterite founders were born, the result has been entirely different. Both communities have recognized as necessary the abandonment of personal posessions and the sharing of all goods and income in common. The Hutterites, economically independent, geographically isolated, and agriculturally self-sufficient, share labor and exchange products rather than cash among themselves. In their urban environment where boundaries are imaginary and cooperative economies rare, the Christians of Reba Place have selected a method of redistribution to support the communitarian effort. Newcomers to the Fellowship transfer their assets, if they have any, to a central fund. Members who work away from the community at salaried jobs hand over their paychecks to the central bookkeeper. Those who have Fellowship jobs contribute labor. Every month the households, families, and individuals receive a living allowance which corresponds to the local welfare allotment. In addition, each mem-

ber is given ten dollars to use charitably any way he chooses.

In contrast to the rigid, hierarchical leadership in a Hutterite colony, authority at Reba is informal. It is believed that God chooses certain individuals to exercise his particular leadership on earth. When the community discerns these individuals, it confirms them as elders and respects them as counselors. Most decisions materialize during group discussions, however, and prayer and Scripture are also sources of guidance. Hilda explained:

"The deciding opinion is not the opinion of the strongest person or the person who can talk best, but the Lord's opinion, what he wants. Often we stop and listen and pray. Out of that, sometimes a word comes to one of us. It can come to anyone in the group. And if it suggests an idea and sounds true to us, we believe that's what the Lord wants us to do and we go ahead with it."

While the Hutterites venerate order, the Rebans applaud spontaneity. They welcomed the recent Pentecostal movement and claim it transformed their "plodding discipleship" into what is now an exuberant, joyful witness of faith. Power for ministry is what they call the Baptism of the Holy Spirit. New members have swelled the community since it began to receive the Spirit's gifts.

After the film *Reba* aired, several widows, single mothers, assorted victims of modern marriage and others who felt simply disconnected and lonely, wrote and called me to ask about Reba Place. Many of them ignored the religious basis of life in the Fellowship, so attractive did it seem as a social experiment. The family at Toad Hall agrees that life in the community is richer than life "in the world."

"Here, even if you're not married you can have a family," said Hilda. "There are children and older people, there are brothers and sisters and mothers and fathers. Life is more rounded and complete. I can see myself living at Reba Place for the rest of my life. I hope I will, because I'd hate to think of getting old in the lonely way many old people today have to suffer."

As a single parent, Melene values the support of the household. "There are many single mothers at Reba Place," she said. "The men of the household fill my daughter's need for fathering

You know, we really didn't expect to have our children come back to us. We thought many of them would go out into the world and choose different ways of life. But it has been a gift, an unexpected gift, to see the first few return to the Fellowship. To see that some of our own children are attracted to the way of life they've grown up in and want to come back to it — as participating adults.

HILDA

and other women help, too, so all aspects of parenting are here in full measure."

"I think most housewives with preschool children face loneliness and frustration," added Jeanne, "but in our household there are more people to help with everything and adults to talk to all day long. It's not just you and the three little children waiting for Daddy to come home. My husband and I are alone together very seldom but it doesn't seem to matter at all because we're united even around that table of fifteen people. The bond of our marriage stretches out to support the whole household. Because the marriage is in Christ, it has been raised to something greater than it was in the smaller setting."

Life at Reba is not easy, however, and without Jesus the "social experiment" would be impossible. When members of the family at Toad Hall speak of their lives in Christ, the word they use again and again is "struggle." Jeanne called it "agonizing." Why is the Christian life so difficult?

"We find that we have to change," explained Hilda. "Not so we'll look better, but because we hurt people we don't want to hurt. It becomes necessary to decide, finally, that I don't want to be a selfish person the rest of my life. That isn't who the Lord wants me to be. I must pray for the Lord to change me."

If Hutterite life is a peaceful avoidance of sin, that of Reba, by comparison, is a prolonged assault on the summit of truth. The corporate faith of Reba Place is assembled from the ruthlessly exposed identities of each of its members, a dangerous strategy made possible only by love and by taking care to distinguish in others the mark of the Creator and in oneself the telltale flaws of the mortal. The goal is to see one another as Jesus sees, to love one another as Jesus loves, to know that all are children of the same father, and to be as children before him.

"You come into a community like this and the real you becomes obvious because you can't hide behind facades," Jeanne said. "Everybody sees who you are and it's awful. You want to hide. But your brothers and sisters accept you and you learn to trust each other."

At Toad Hall rebuke and reconciliation are common elements of the atmosphere, but special efforts are made to expose and solve problems at frequent evening meetings of the adults of the household. I was the subject of one of these meetings and I can testify to the searing candor with which they are conducted.

When I first began visiting religious groups, my own spirit was so empty and my experience of God so small, that whatever I was taught I accepted wholeheartedly. No one could doubt my sincerity because my enthusiasm was obvious. Eventually I came to take it for granted that people would trust me.

A few years later when I visited Reba Place, I listened to religious ideas more critically, but I assumed that the sincerity of my admiration was still apparent to everyone. Unfortunately it was not apparent to the Christians of Toad Hall. At a meeting of the household, Jeanne told me she distrusted, even feared me, that my honesty seemed questionable, no less my motives for making films. Others agreed. For three hours they prodded and soothed me until I became much more frank and open, not only with them but with myself, about my work and my beliefs, my pride and my fears.

A month later when we filmed a meeting at Toad Hall, there were other issues:

"What I've learned today is that I'm not a pacifist," Jeanne told the group. She and Melene had quarreled about disciplining the children. "Maybe you don't feel this way, Melene, but I felt you attacked me and I think I have the right to fight back if somebody attacks me first. But when you said, just in passing, 'You know, Jeanne and I have had an extraordinarily good relationship as mothers together,' something changed within me and I think we were both able to allow God's love to come through each of us to the other and to be reconciled."

David had a problem of another sort: "My relationship with the Lord isn't really personal," he complained. "I don't know if I ever had a real desire to have a personal relationship with him. That's always seemed to me the kind of thing all those phony pious people do. I can't get into any kind of encounter with him. I might as well be a rock."

Hilda offered a prayer for David: "Father give this gift not only to David but to me as well. To any of us who want to know you better and to love you more."

Later Jeanne said, "Nobody has what David is looking for because what he is looking for is his own unique relationship to the Lord. All that is yet to be unfolded."

As the meeting continued, the members of the household disposed of each issue candidly, humbly, sometimes a bit ruthlessly and always finally by giving it up to God. In conclusion, they prayed:

"Thank you, Father, for being with the people of this house today, for bringing us together in love and spirit. Thank you for brothers and sisters with whom we can share our life, who can speak to us and sustain us at all times. Continue to teach us your ways, Father, and help us to be more like your son Jesus. In his name we pray. Amen."

Jesus said, "If you are bringing your offering to the altar and there remember that your brother has something against you, go and be reconciled with your brother first . . ." (Matt. 5:23–24)

No one loves God who distrusts his brother and no one trusts his brother who does not know himself. Surely self-knowledge is the most strenuous of humilities. Because that truth is always poised between pride and abasement, the pursuit of it must be arrow sure and tortoise steady. To the monk or the Yogi, the quest, as stated, is vain. What could one hope to know but the God within? The genius of Reba perceives that all truths are God's truths. Thus Hilda can say, "When I know who I really am, Jesus is as real to me as if I saw him standing here right beside me."

Reconciled and loving, the members of the Fellowship gather once a month to celebrate the Lord's Supper. No one eats the holy food who is not in harmony with his brothers and sisters. This night is free of confessions and apologies. There are smiles and embraces and the giddiness of joy. Following truth may be a wearying task, but the one who is truth promises strength and, in the end, a river of peace.

I've been living communally for fifteen years now. I think I got hooked on it while I was in Europe. I was working on a publication team there and for five years we lived together and worked together and ate together and so on. When I came back to the States, I became part of the ordinary church life where you go, you know, once a week on Sunday and maybe there's some activity in between. Nobody really shares deeply with one another what's going on in their hearts, nor do they really want to be shared with. I felt a difference, a loneliness, moving from one to the other. When the opportunity came to become part of Reba Place, that's what I did. And it's been wonderful.

HILDA

Lighthouse Ranch

A light wind sprinkles sand over a circle of Bibles waiting on the beach above tideline. The fog bloats their pages. Newborn Christians, baptized in foam where the ocean wall shatters and hisses in to shore, stagger toward the beach, shouting praises against the roar of the Pacific. They have died in the salt water and live again in Jesus.

The joy of new birth is repeated endlessly at the Lighthouse Ranch as each young Christian discovers that his life, once confused and indifferent, now is certain, enthusiastic, and purposeful. It is filled with love. So powerful and so positive is the transformation, he knows it is a miracle performed by the Lord.

If a newcomer witnesses the miracle taking place in others and wishes to experience it himself, he must give up all attempts to "understand" Jesus. Conversion is not an achievement of the intellect, but a simple act of faith. It requires the candidate to step into the unknown, confidently trusting that the Lord will receive him. The experienced Christians explain this necessity to the newcomer again and again. They urge him to do it, to accept the Lord. When he finally takes that first step, he understands at last what could never have been described and he becomes as enthusiastic and single-minded about following Jesus as the people who may originally have confused or repelled him.

Sarah recalled her experience:

"I was living in San Francisco and I was married and had a child and we sold dope for a living. It was really hard on me and I just had to go somewhere, so I went to the ranch and hated it. All the Christians were, you know, telling me about the love of the Lord all the time, and I just told them what I thought of the Lord and that the Bible was a myth and that I'd studied it in mythological studies in college and I told them what I thought of Christianity. But they said, 'Well, we love you. You can stay here as long as you want.'

"Then one night I was in the chapel with a brother named Timothy and two other people, and Timothy said, 'Let's pray.' And so we sat down on the floor, just the four of us, and he started praying. It was dark and there was a fire going and a candle and it was very beautiful. I was feeling really peaceful and wonderful, you know, just the peace of the moment. I was listening to Timothy out of the corner of my mind and he said, 'Ask Jesus into your heart.' And I thought, 'Well, sure, I'll ask Jesus into my heart,' and it happened. I mean it wasn't any big effort or anything. I didn't go up before the church or cry. I just said, 'Yes, that's it.' I asked Jesus into my heart and he came. And he hasn't left."

So real is the experience of the Lord that Lighthouse Christians are convinced the only way to live is as his disciple, which for them means to convert others. They waste no time telling visitors the "good news" of Jesus Christ.

Before filming at the commune, I had a talk with the Christians about the film crew. "Even though they are heathens," I warned, "please don't disturb them at their work."

Back in 1966, I was living at home in a wealthy, elite neighborhood of Los Angeles. Afternoons my friends and I used to hang out in the parking lot of a shopping center. We'd open all our car doors and turn on our stereo tapes and have a party in the parking lot while we figured out what we were going to do that night. One day two Christians came up and started sharing with us about Jesus Christ and how he changed their lives, how they didn't need to use drugs any more, how they'd found fulfillment in the Lord. We all chuckled among ourselves — it seemed so foolish — but there was nothing else to do that night so we got loaded and went over to their place. They rapped to us about the Lord for a long time. They asked us, "How many of you want to give your life to Jesus Christ?" And of course no one was ready to hang his life up yet. I thought my life was pretty good. I was having a good time. I had my lowered car, my stereo tapes, all the girls I could handle, all the money I wanted, and all the dope I could possibly use. I was dealing then. I was just cruising around — the king of my little town. And the Christian said, "Man, you'd want something better if you could have it, wouldn't you?" And because I was a very logical person and had a very high I.Q., I said, "Well, sure. I'm no dummy. I'll take it, especially if it's free." I thought I'd just knock Christianity out of my bag of tricks and just go on to the next thing. So I asked Jesus to come into my heart and forgive my sins, figuring if it works, it works. And if it doesn't, it doesn't. And six years later it's never, never turned off at all.

RON

On the way to California I explained to the crew (who were on their first assignment for the television series of *Religious America*) that some of our subjects would be interested in the crew's salvation. That, to tell the truth, the Lighthouse Christians thought the Lord was sending them to Loleta specifically to be "saved." If the crew were not certain what that meant, they soon found out.

As we drove into the ranch in our rented truck, a bevy of excited Christians rushed out to meet us. The cynical sound man and the lighting expert were captured in embraces as they stepped from the truck. "Have you met the Lord?" demanded the Christians.

The crew quickly realized that they were safe from the proselytizers only while they appeared to be working, and they became ingenious at simulating activity. Never has film and sound equipment been cared for more scrupulously. When they needed a rest, the crew hid in the truck or crept off to the beach. The Christians were careful not to interfere with what appeared to be work, but they watched with feline patience and vigilance for an opportunity to pounce on an idle stranger and urge him to accept Jesus.

The humor of the situation was lost on both factions. Several of the crew members thought the Christians were demented; some vowed to go on location for only children's shows in the future. The Christians never ceased to be friendly and kind, but they could see no reason why the crew members should be unwilling to forget their jobs, their sinful lives, accept the Lord, and join the commune. By the time we left, none of the crew was anxious to stay behind, although one of the leaders of the commune felt sure that Joan Carlson, associate producer, was "inches away" from accepting Jesus. He speculated that Joan would start speaking in tongues and receive the baptism even before we got out of the commune driveway.

One wonders who but Jesus could be running the ranch? The fervor seems constantly on the verge of exploding into chaos, but somehow the garden always gets weeded, the goats get milked, and food for a dozen extra mouths turns up.

There were two leaders at the ranch when I visited: one to

While we were filming at the Lighthouse Ranch, Nancy and David decided to get married and announced their engagement at a church gathering. Later they explained:
David: *I felt that Nancy was something special. One night after church I asked her if she wanted to go for a walk. The sky was clear and the stars were out. The Lord was there.*
Nancy: *David said, "I've been thinking about you all day." And I said, "Me, too".*
David: *I just told her that I felt he was drawing us together.*
Nancy: *It's as if it was the first time I ever had a boy friend, like I'm just a child. It's so new. After two weeks he finally held my hand.*
David: *Together we'll just talk to the Lord like there's three of us there. It's different from any other kind of man-woman relationship because it's founded on Christ.*

manage the practical affairs of the commune, the other to guide the community on the spiritual path. They were both chosen by the community because the Lord seemed to grace them with the understanding and wisdom necessary to serve their brothers and sisters.

The economics of the ranch are simple: share what the Lord provides. For cash, the commune peddles doughnuts door to door in Loleta ("Good morning, brother, do you know Jesus?"); it prints an advertising newspaper which includes the "good news"; and it sells leather belts with Scriptures gracefully tooled inside or outside as you prefer.

The theology of the Lighthouse Christians is equally simple. The Holy Bible is the root and the flower of their belief. They use it to make the most basic decision or to adorn the most trivial speech. They recognize no darkness which the Old and New Testaments cannot illuminate, no ignorance they cannot dispel.

Every evening a hundred or more Christians gather for worship in one of the old Coast Guard buildings near the beach. Prayer, testimony, music, speaking in tongues, prophecy, bible study, and preaching combine freely and unpredictably late into the night. The influence of Pentecostalism is obvious in the spontaneity of the prayer and the presence of the charismatic gifts, but no one is pressured to receive the Baptism of the Holy Spirit or to speak in tongues.

"Give us a song, Sarah!" a brother calls out and Sarah, blushing, nods to the young man with a guitar who sits next to her. They sing a duet, a love song for Jesus, and the audience links arms and joins in the refrain. Faces upturned to the paint-peeled ceiling, they see only beauty. In spite of the cold dampness which creeps up from the beach, they feel only warmth. As the song ends, random couples, even strangers embrace like reunited lovers.

The excitement of loving Jesus, of loving each other, of simply loving more and more, never slackens at the ranch. There is literally a smile on every face. God's name is praised everywhere. Once when I was enjoying momentary privacy in the shelter of a bathroom, I answered a knock on the door by calling out, "there's someone in here." "Praise the Lord!" came the answer.

Sarah commented on the mood of the ranch:

"Jesus said, 'hereby will the world know that you are my disciples by the love you have one to another.' And that's how we can live in a communal situation. One hundred twenty people living on five acres, in three or four homes, it's ridiculous. No one would try it, it wouldn't work unless we had the Lord. Because our personalities would clash, our needs would clash, and we wouldn't be able to make it together. I just know it. I've been to other communes that weren't Christian and they don't have the same kind of feeling, the same unity.

"The best thing about communal living is it's like rocks in a tumbler. They just bang the raw edges off each other and they come out smooth stones. And that's how you come out of the ranch — a very strong Christian in a very short period of time."

Many of the young Christians remain at the ranch and become part of the family of one hundred twenty. Others are graduated from it as new men and women and return to their families or to school, to a church community, and often to some kind of Christian ministry. The ranch's population is always changing as lost souls wander in and converts emerge. Its essential virtue is freedom: freedom to leave in anger and return for love, freedom to express the joy and amazement of Christian devotion, freedom to follow a path prepared by the Lord.

Lighthouse Christianity is no fad or passing fancy. Not everyone who passes through the ranch is touched by it, but for those who are a change takes place. Nancy spoke of the change in her life:

"I had a farm, I had a goat, I had dogs and cats. I had a lot of men and relationships with all different kinds of people. I had everything, everything I've ever wanted. Still something inside my heart cried out.

"I saw that everything, my whole life, was for nothing. All the things in it were incomplete. I realized it, I knew it, and I saw that Jesus loved me and I just opened up my heart and said, 'I want you in my life.'

"And all of the burdens were lifted up to him. He took me in his hands and just lifted them all away and I was his."

Before I became a Christian a warrant was issued for my arrest for the sale of drugs. So about three weeks after my conversion I went down to San Francisco to turn myself in. I thought they were going to say, "What a wonderful girl" and let me go, and just say, "come to court some day."

Well, I got there and they put me in jail. They tossed me in a cell all by myself. This matron was bullying me around and people were swearing left and right. I felt alone. I wasn't crying but I was a little worried. There were no Christians around. The place was cold, damp, this women's jail.

There were no windows and the beds had no blankets, just plastic over them. And I just called on the Lord. They wouldn't let me have a Bible, so I started singing — I had to be in his arms again. I sang every song I had learned since becoming a Christian, over and over again. I'd sleep and then sing some more.

One time I stopped singing in the middle of a verse of "Amazing Grace" and I heard somebody weeping in another cell. The people in the jail were getting so touched. All I was doing was hanging on for dear life, singing, and people were getting touched by the Lord through it.

And that's when I learned that my salvation didn't depend on living at the Lighthouse Ranch or going to church or reading the Bible. My salvation is in the Lord.

SARAH

Guru Ram Das Ashram

When I perform the exercises of Tantric Yoga, I look into my partner's eyes and she is absolutely beautiful. As I sit in the proper position, I feel totally divine. Then all of a sudden, I begin to feel pain. When it becomes almost excruciating, I say to myself, "This is heaven." But another voice inside me speaks up: "If this is heaven, how come it hurts?" And I reply, "Do you think there's no trouble in heaven? How boring it would be if there weren't a little pain."

GURUSHABD SINGH

"When I started wearing a turban three and a half years ago," recalled Gurushabd Singh, "my parents and all my relatives and many of my friends were shocked. But I wore it nevertheless. The turban symbolized to me a new way of life, one that was lived without fear, in total honesty and service to God."

"There is but one God, truth is his name, great is his indescribable wisdom," proclaims the Sikh religion Gurushabd has chosen to follow. The Sikh sages add, "Millions are the men who give millions of descriptions of him." This recognition (and tolerance) of multiple perceptions of divinity is as characteristic of the religions of India as its corollary, "he who tries to describe God shall repent."

Sikhism was founded in the mid-fifteenth century in northern India by Guru Nanak. The God praised by Nanak combines elements of both Islam and Hinduism; he is creative and sustaining as well as immanent and ineffable. To know him fully in his formless totality is to know one's true nature and to see the ultimate reality beyond the veil of illusion which is the world of the senses. Meditation and Kundalini Yoga are part of the Sikh method for achieving this knowledge.

The American Kundalini Yogis, as they call themselves, are not unique in adopting religious beliefs and practices from India. What is special about them, besides their gentle sense of humor, is the unity and discipline of their way of life, the fullness of the religion they practice and, at the same time, their openness to visions of life and God other than their own. In its American version the religion is informal and undogmatic. It requires an attitude more than a belief.

Sikhism began to grow in the United States in the late sixties, a time when many spiritually underfed young people began to investigate Eastern philosophies. The communes where it is practiced are called "ashrams," a word which means "home of the guru" and denotes their function as places of learning.

At the Guru Ram Das Ashram in Montague, Massachusetts, a dozen or more men and women live with a common purpose. Gurushabd explained: "We try to live in a very sensible way by feeling what God's will is and becoming one with that. Our religion has no ritual merely for its own sake. Everything we do is practical. All the yoga, the meditation, the vegetarian diet, the way we live together: it all gives us a feeling of peace and puts us in harmony with the whole cosmos."

Superficially the ashram's style of life resembles that of the Lighthouse Ranch. "We try to live selflessly," Gurushabd continued, "We try to give each other as much love and understanding and compassion as we can. Sometimes that creates sort of a pressure cooker environment. Your ego and your own petty preferences have to slip away for the house to function smoothly."

When it comes to theology, the Kundalinis and the young Christians are worlds apart. For the Yogis, Jesus is not the "one way"; he is simply a wise man. God has no quality and he has every quality. He creates, he organizes, and he destroys all that exists. He asks the devotee to give up false perceptions, not false gods. He does not reward a good man with Heaven or a bad one with Hell, after a single life on earth. Instead he offers the hope of release from an endless cycle of rebirth. Nor does the Sikh God punish wrongdoers. "By our actions, we draw him near or far" is the simple statement of Sikh morality.

"There is no sin," maintains Gurushabd. "There can't be any sin. There are only lower and higher actions according to your own consciousness and your own abilities. You try always to do the highest thing, but when you fail there's no guilt. That's really unnecessary. Guilt is a waste of time. To be guilty is not to be living in the present."

Gurushabd Singh is the leader of the Guru Ram Das Ashram.

He and several thousand other Kundalinis are students of Yogi Bhajan. Gurushabd is quick to emphasize that they respect Yogi Bhajan as a teacher but do not consider him divine. In Gurushabd's words he is "just a man who knows how to live perfectly."

Yogiji, as they call him affectionately, is a spiritual father whose sayings are heard often in conversation. "Yogiji says you shouldn't sit on the bare ground. . . . Yogiji tells us the woman is the giver of happiness." Small framed photographs of Yogiji's face peer out of shrine-like corners of the ashram.

The summer and winter solstices are occasions for Kundalini powwows. White-clad, turbanned Yogis overflow old Postal Service vans and Volkswagen buses as they trundle to the chosen spot from all directions to spend the longest and shortest days of the year with Yogi Bhajan. Everyone is welcome to hear the Yogi's teachings, and currently he is fairly accessible, but in daily practice the members of the ashram look to Gurushabd for guidance.

The Yogis practice a "dharma," a righteous way of living. Guru Ram Das, a sixteenth-century successor to Nanak, advised his disciples to rise before the coming of the light, bathe, and await the dawn while meditating on the true nature of God. The Yogis follow his prescription. They abandon the comfort of their beds at 2:30 each morning and jolt their bodies awake with cold showers. Then they begin the rigorous Kundalini Yoga exercises. Gracefully and thoroughly, the Yogis flex their muscles, bend their limbs, stretch their spines. They snort and puff like seals at an air hole. Proper breathing is essential to the correct performance of the Yoga. By learning to control his body and to cradle his breath, the Yogi hopes to master the five passions (ego, attachment, lust, anger, and greed) and become free from their bondage. Like the other disciplines he practices, this one helps to release the mind from the grip of the ego and raise it toward a higher consciousness of the ultimate reality.

The extraordinary exercises last for several hours and conclude with chanting and meditation. At last comes breakfast, one of the Kundalinis' two meals a day, and then it is time to work.

Some members of the ashram have regular jobs in the com-

When I fall victim to my own ingratitude, when I think that what I decide or do is important, then I've totally stepped off the path. It's only when I live in gratitude and when I realize that God is giving me the breath I breathe that everything becomes serene and service is a joy.

GURUSHABD SINGH

119

munity, some are students, others teach Yoga, and some work at home at the ashram. The important thing, say the Kundalinis, is to do your work graciously and to be mindful only of the process and not the result. "Karma Yoga," the performance of work with the devotion of ritual, teaches that actions performed for their own sake have consequences in the next illusory world: the fruit of such actions is unwanted rebirth. Actions performed in obedience to duty without attachment to their effects bring the performer closer to that knowledge of God which will transport him across the ocean of many lives to dwell eternally in formless truth.

"In my life," explained Gurushabd, "situations just present themselves and I try to do exactly what's necessary. If it's necessary to eat a salad I do that, and if it's necessary to go out and weed the garden I do that."

Sat Kartar agreed: "Instead of doing a job because I want to do it, or because someone obliges me to do it, I simply perform my duty with gratitude and love and I dedicate the fruits of my actions to God."

"It doesn't really matter what you do in this life, as long as you do it with the right attitude," added Sat Nam Kaur. "I chant to myself while I work because it helps me to develop that attitude."

The members of the Guru Ram Das Ashram are young. Many of them began meditation or Yoga classes simply as an "exercise" and only later became tuned to the larger spiritual dimension. Gurushabd laughed as he recalled his introduction to Yoga: "Before I took up Yoga, my life was funky and miserable. I used to refer to it as an existential choo-choo train going on into the wilderness. One day a flyer came in my mail advertising Yoga classes at something called the 'Institute for Self-Satisfaction.' Well, the name sounded so bogus and so silly that it appealed to my sense of humor, so I went to a class and loved it. The Yoga teacher completely mystified me, but the exercises made me feel great. I became his student and later a student of Yogi Bhajan."

A follower of Sikhism is a "student," not a "convert." He exchanges his old name for a braver and more beautiful one, but his old and new lives are not abruptly discontinuous. The names and

The mind and the body are connected. The exercises we do in the morning prepare us for the day; they get the body working perfectly. And when your body is working that way, your emotions also fall into place and your life becomes calm and even. In every movement and every gesture we're practicing how to relate to the world and to our highest consciousness.

Kundalini Yoga is just a technique. It requires a lot of energy and a lot of perseverance and it has a lot of fun in it, too. We call ourselves Yogis, we call ourselves Sikhs, we call ourselves just plain folks.

GURUSHABD SINGH

121

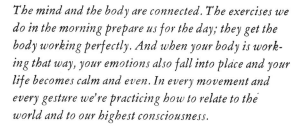

the turbans are misleadingly exotic. "Are your parents still shocked by the turban?" I asked Gurushabd.

"Oh, no," he answered. "They don't even notice it."

The atmosphere of the ashram is perpetually serene. At times it is almost somnolent. Because the Kundalinis sleep only four or five hours a night, they waste no energy during the day. They live together as actors in the same tranquil dream. Meditation rests their bodies and purifies their minds. It is vital to the knowledge they seek.

"I meditate to get myself centered," said Gurushabd. "Meditation clears my mind of distractions. When my mind and my body are at rest, I tune into the highest consciousness I can muster at the moment."

Sat Kartar commented: "When I meditate, I don't experience such a mystical inexpressible feeling. I feel clean, I feel buoyant, light and totally relieved. No problems confront me at that moment, and everything around me is beautiful."

"Sat Nam," murmur the Kundalinis both in greeting and in praise. It means "truth is the manifestation of God's holy name." To pronounce the words is to declare one's love for God and to affirm that "truth is my existence." Meditations and Yoga exercises are often based on the repetition of the words Sat Nam.

"When we do the exercises in Kundalini Yoga, we say Sat Nam with each breath," explains Gurushabd Kaur. "When you do that you link your breath to God's truth. Without God's meditation on me, which is constant and perfect, I wouldn't even be breathing. He is the breath inside me. If I can use every breath to tell the truth and to praise him in gratitude, then I am one with him."

The Yogis do not seek the enlightenment of Buddhism or salvation in the Christian sense. They try to live in the present as perfectly as they possibly can. They intend their lives to be positive and dedicated to the service of God, believing that "to be in a positive state of mind is to be in a meditative state." In the Kundalini cosmology, God and man are not merely inseparable, they are identical. The Yogi's ardent wish is to live in awareness of his unity with all creation. Gurushabd explained.

"Yoga means union, and the union we seek is with the universe. When you feel that you are a separate little self, alone and untouched by the world around you, you are deceived. That is a state of ignorance. That's when you can feel afraid.

"But when you lose that feeling, when you realize that you are connected to every single thing in the universe, that it could not be perfect without you, then you become brave. You don't feel as if situations are outside you, that people are separate from you. You are no longer trapped in your personality. It feels like being in love with every molecule in the universe and with every breath of air, and that's a very blissful feeling."

Gurushabd and his wife, Gurushabd Kaur, call their marriage an exchange of divine love. Their infant son, they tell you, is not really their child. "He is God's child," they insist. Their family beautifies the ashram as the marriage beautifies their lives.

"When I got married," said Gurushabd Kaur, "my teacher asked me, 'Do you know who it is you are marrying?' I just looked at her with a strange expression and she whispered in my ear, 'It's God.' When you relate to a person, what you relate to is the God in him. You try to transcend all personality and just relate to that part of him that is God."

A visitor to the ashram soon becomes oblivious to the turbans, the exotic food, and the unfamiliar customs. The Kundalinis are so serene, so friendly that one feels immediately relaxed and comfortable with them. Why not be happy, their attitude suggests. Unhappiness, like guilt, is a waste of time. As Gurushabd Kaur puts it, "You can choose to be positive or to be negative, and it takes the same amount of energy to be either one."

Gurushabd continues, "There is no reason for life not to be simple. Everything has been given to us: a way to live and a way to grow. Nothing in our lives is without a purpose. We try to live so beautifully that God will come and dwell with us because we are so attractive to him. When I'm happy I feel one with God and His creation. It is neither above me nor beneath me. I am aware of it at that point and that's totally delicious."

V   The Personal Voice

P.O.W.

COMMANDER MCDANIEL:

On May 19, 1967, flying from the deck of the U.S.S. *Enterprise,* I piloted one of twenty-six aircraft that attacked a target deep within the city of Hanoi. It was my eighty-first combat mission over North Vietnam. I was hit by a Russian-built surface-to-air missile, and on impact I lost all hydraulic controls. The aircraft pitched down in a twenty-degree dive and started burning. We stayed with it for about seventy seconds in order to reach a mountainous area where we thought we might have a chance to evade the enemy. About two thousand feet above the mountains, my right seater, Lt. James Kelly Patterson, ejected. I ejected one second behind him and parachuted into the jungle of North Vietnam.

MRS. MCDANIEL:

Several nights after Red was shot down, I realized that he was either going to die in that jungle or he was going to be a prisoner of war. It was a very frantic time for me; at first, I wasn't even able to pray. I fell on my knees by my bed and whispered, "Help." That was all I could say. I went to bed that night and dreamed that Red was in a jungle and was being attacked by wild animals. I woke up in the middle of the dream and without really thinking I reached over for the Bible beside my bed. I opened my Bible to Psalm 91 and I read: "He that dwelleth in the secret place of the most high, shall abide under the shadow of the Almighty." And the Psalm goes on and describes lions and adders and wild beasts. And then it says, "He shall call upon me and I will answer him." And I knew that God was with Red.

COMMANDER MCDANIEL:

My first night in the jungle, I asked myself and I asked God over and over again, "Why me? Why did this happen to me?" Well, after I got to the prison and saw people dying, guys being tortured — my roommate was lying there with really critical wounds — I began to count my blessings. At that point I realized things could be far worse for me. I acknowledged the fact that God was there with me and trusted that his will would be done. At night under my mosquito net, I'd pray for my survival and for my family. I'd thank God for protecting them and I'd pray that he would bring peace and reunite us.

MRS. MCDANIEL:

Four days after he was shot down, I was told that my husband was presumed to be a prisoner of war. That was the last official word I had for three years. I didn't know what to think. We lived in a state of limbo for those three years, the children and I. They would ask, "Where is Daddy?" and I'd say, "I don't know." It worried me that I couldn't answer their questions, and I was desperate to know if, in fact, Red was in one of those camps. But because we were so close in our relationship, our spirits were so close, I was sure I would know it if he died. Even if it happened in the middle of a jungle somewhere, I would know — some way — if Red were no longer alive. For three years I learned to live day by day. I turned the situation over to God.

COMMANDER MCDANIEL:

To me, communication with my fellow prisoners was all important.

It was our life's blood in North Vietnam. It was a risk because when we were caught, we were tortured. When I was first called up for interrogation, I knew it was going to be a pretty gruesome ordeal. I prayed to God for the strength and courage to deal with it — to protect the information I had, to survive or, if I did die, to go decently. I just gave my life to God. I've always been very competitive, very proud. I knew that when it was all over, I'd go back to my room and live with my roommates and I'd have to account for my actions. So I hung on as long as I could. After the third or fourth day of being beaten with a fan belt, I began hallucinating a little bit. I remember very vividly hearing, twenty-four hours a day, the song "White Christmas." It would just fade in and fade out. I don't know why I heard that one song. At one point I became irrational and attacked a guard. I was beaten very severely and put into the ropes for several hours. During the torture, my arm was broken at the elbow, and because of the ropes I lost the use of my hands for eight months. My legs swelled up with infection from the open wounds caused by the beatings and the leg irons. I lost thirty or forty pounds in eight days. When they brought me back to my room, all the men in the building watched — men who had seen me every day for months. No one was able to recognize me. They had no idea who I was until much later when I was able to communicate.

MRS. MCDANIEL:

Sometimes I wondered if I were over-protecting the children. How much should I talk about the situation? How hard should I try not to talk about it? I had the feeling that Leslie, who was very young, hardly remembered Red at all — I just didn't mention him to her very much. I felt it was easier for her not to hear about it all the time. I began to wonder if she knew she even had a father. And then one night when she was having dinner at a friend's house, she watched her friend's father (he's a good friend of ours) pile spaghetti on his plate and she asked, "Do you always eat that much?" And he said, "Sure." And she said, "You know, my Dad never gets enough to eat." Well, when he told me this story I realized that she

was very aware of what was going on. She was about six at the time.

COMMANDER MCDANIEL:

In late 1969, after the treatment began to get better, they came around and asked us all if we wanted to write home. Of course, we had all composed a letter in our minds, we were proud of that. We had no idea whether or not the letters would be mailed, but it was nice to be allowed to write. I wrote a letter to my wife in December, 1969 — I later learned it reached her in May of '70.

MRS. MCDANIEL:

He wrote, "Dear Dorothy, Michael, David, Leslie: My health is good in all respects. No permanent injuries. You are my inspiration. Children — work, study, play hard. Help each other and Mommy. Be strong for our reunion." And then he tells us that he loves us and signs it. I could hardly believe it was real. This, this one piece of paper we had wanted so much. For at least a month after the letter came, I would wake up in the middle of the night and think, "Did I really get a letter?" And I'd go and find it and read it and touch it to see if it really was authentic. And it really was. It's practically worn out.

COMMANDER MCDANIEL:

I got one letter from Leslie when she was about seven years old. You know what she said? She said, "I hope you are having a nice time. Because we are having a very, very nice time." So I went back to the room and told everyone what Leslie wrote — they got a big kick out of that.

I always tried to be optimistic. Many men were despondent; I tried to prop up their morale. Every time I heard a good rumor I remembered it, and every time I heard a bad one I'd bury it. I tried to feel that we were always within several months of going home. We had a daily prayer club. We prayed every day that we would be home for Christmas. It went on year after year.

Each Sunday, right from the beginning, we would have a very

short, simple church service. We'd tap on the walls all the way down the building, six or seven rooms, and then we would say in unison the Lord's prayer, the Twenty-third Psalm, or the Beatitudes and a silent prayer. After we moved to the Hanoi Hilton, there were fifty-seven of us in one room and the senior officer came over and asked me if I would consider being the chaplain. I told him I thought other men were better qualified, knew more scripture, could do a better job, but he said, "No, I'd like you to be the chaplain." So I organized a Sunday church service. We even had a choir of twelve or fifteen people. The Viet Cong didn't like this and kept interrupting us, but we knew we were on firm ground and decided to sing at the top of our voices for a couple of days. We sang "God Bless America," "Onward Christian Soldiers," and all the other hymns we could remember. When we ran out of those, we started singing Notre Dame fight songs, any song we could think of. But the purpose was to achieve the right to have a church service. The result was that many men were tortured and put into isolation, but we got what we wanted, a fifteen-minute church service.

MRS. MCDANIEL:

I heard someone say once that until you have suffered, you don't know all that God wants you to know. I don't know if that's true for everybody — God works in very personal and individual ways with people. But it was true for me. I learned to accept God's will and to trust that whatever he allows to happen in our lives is ultimately going to work for our good.

COMMANDER MCDANIEL:

Just before leaving for Vietnam, in fact the very night before I left, my wife and I were lying in bed and she asked me if I were ready with God to die. I felt then that I was not ready. But after some of the tortures, the deprivations and injuries, there were times when I would have welcomed death. I prepared myself to die, if necessary, if that were God's will. I feel that God was with

me and still is and is with most people, that there is a purpose for men to die as well as for men to live.

MRS. MCDANIEL:

Finally the thing really happened, he was released. Someone telephoned me at three o'clock in the morning and said, "Your husband's plane is in the air. He is now on his way to the Philippines." When the plane landed, we watched it on television and when he walked down the ramp, I just dissolved into tears. The children had to tell me what he did. I never saw anything except his face. I just can't describe to you how we felt when we saw him. The joy was so tremendous, no words can express it.

COMMANDER MCDANIEL'S PRAYER:

Dear heavenly father, at the close of another day we come to you to thank you for our many blessings — for our health, our well-being, and our reunion. Thank you for my wonderful wife and the greatest blessing of all, the children. Thank you for the protection that you gave them during those many long years in which we lost much, but we also gained much. We pray we shall never forget those long, difficult moments and we know that more will be forthcoming. Give us the strength as you did in the past to overcome all tribulations. Thank you again for uniting us and for the protection and shelter that you gave my family during my long absence. Please continue to bless us as we continue to pray: "The Lord is my shepherd, I shall not want; he maketh me to lie down in green pastures. He leadeth me beside the still waters; he restoreth my soul. He leadeth me in the paths of righteousness for his name's sake. Yea, though I walk through the valley of the shadow of death, I will fear no evil; for thou art with me; thy rod and thy staff they comfort me. Thou preparest a table before me in the presence of mine enemies; thou anointest my head with oil, my cup runneth over. Surely goodness and mercy shall follow me all the days of my life; and I shall dwell in the house of the Lord for ever."

Jim

I was born in Dorchester, a part of Boston. It was a pretty rough neighborhood and there was plenty of fighting. I had nine brothers and two sisters. With such a large family, you really have to battle. I mean, if you want the head chair you've got to fight for it. I'm not one for turning the other cheek — if you do, the other guy is going to lay you out.

I was brought up Catholic. My father used to walk behind us to make sure we went to church and to Sunday school. Of course, he didn't go. My mother did.

Looking back, I'm glad he forced us. It really taught me a lot about life. But now, as for going to church — I really can't see it. Because if you believe in God you don't have to show people by going to church or kneeling down and praying. If you've got that inner feeling, you know you've got it.

After graduation I entered the service and became an Air Force mechanic for four years. When I got out I got a job as a rubbish man and I've been doing that for over ten years. My father was a rubbish man before I was even thought of.

The most important time of my life was when I met Andrea and decided to marry her. She was visiting my sister when I came home on leave and it was love at first sight, believe me. The first time I tried to get a date with her, she wouldn't go out with me. I think she was afraid of me because I was older than she was. Finally she said yes and it was great — we took a ride down to Cape Cod and wouldn't you know, my car radiator steamed up and I had to pull over. It was no fakin'. Of course, she didn't believe it. She thought I was pulling the old break-down trick with the car. "Take me home!" she was yelling at me. "I can't!" I kept telling her. We never did get down to the Cape.

We got married in '64. It was a challenge — something I'd looked forward to — being married and raising a family, caring and showing them that I could support them. When I bought my house, I loved it; I thought it was really something. It was mine, all mine. And you buy land to go with it. It's great, but it's a lot of responsibility. Supporting a family nowadays is rough, but I knew what I was in for.

The best part was having the babies. We had our first son in '65 and another one a year later. Then the girl came along in '68 and another boy a year after that. Andrea says no more so I guess that's it, but I'd love to have more. I think everybody would if you didn't have to worry about food and clothes and medical bills starving you, but the way life is now, you can't afford to have more children.

There's nothing like holding a newborn. Nothing like a woman being pregnant, too. Something real beautiful in them. Their face, their eyes, their whole shape and outlook on life when they're carrying is beautiful. You know that there's life there and it's part of you and her both.

Andrea is my sweetheart. It's hard for her to be with the kids all day and all night and I'm a son of a gun myself at times, but she never lets us down, come hell or high water. She's really something special.

Used to be she was bothered by my being a rubbish man, but I told her a man's gotta work and that's as good a job as anybody else's. Now she's used to it. It pays good and she knows I'm a hard-working man.

People who say my job is dirty — they're right. It is dirty. But it has to be done and people like me do it. It's not the nicest job, but I enjoy it. I was brought up doing hard work — I was always chopping and sawing wood for our family's furnace. Before I even learned to walk, my father put a piece of wood in my hand and said, go put it in the fire — and I've been working ever since.

There's nothing you have to know in rubbish. If you want to work, you get out there and work and that's it. It's hard work. At the end of the day, you go home bone-tired. You sleep good — if you don't it's your own fault.

You can enjoy yourself in any kind of work. You can work in the sewers and still have a good time. You gotta have a sense of humor to do a job like mine, otherwise you get grouchy. We have a lady on the route who lowers candy out her window for us because we put her barrels away for her. She's old and can't do it. Every Tuesday like clockwork, down comes a bucket of candy. It's just something to say thank you for putting the barrels back. That makes you feel good, you know. I don't even know anything about her. I only see her at the window, wave hello, wave goodbye.

Of course, sometimes you feel down, you feel like staying in bed. Every working man gets that feeling once in a while. Monday's the worst, but once you get up and breathe that morning air, it's like a new day to you. It wouldn't be me if I had nothing to do.

The best part of the day is going home to the family. When I see my kids I know I'm home. They drop everything and come running to hug me; they're overjoyous when Daddy's home from work. That's what I love. I did the same to my father when he got home — run down the street to meet him. My kids grab me around the legs and don't let me go until I lift them up. It's the end of the day and it's wonderful.

I fool with the kids pretty rough. If I was too soft, they wouldn't come back for more. They enjoy letting out all their emotions and once they start roughhousing they really go all out. You can't let yourself worry about them getting hurt. If I worried every time they climbed a tall pine tree they'd see that I was afraid for them and they'd be leery going up.

I love life — it's something to be enjoyed. I'm scared of death, aren't you? I like to walk through cemeteries and look at the headstones, it makes me feel great that I'm alive. When you see a five-week old baby lying next to a person who lived to be a hundred and five, it makes you wonder why some people die young and others live for such a long time. I think of what their lives must have been like and I wonder what struck them down. Death is a part of living. I know I'm going to die some day, it's inevitable. I just don't want it to come any sooner than it's supposed to. But who knows? Tomorrow I may just whoosh! and that will be it.

You can't say I'm not religious. I am religious — in my own way. I may not go to church, yes, but I'm not a heathen. I enjoy myself and I just take life as it comes. God is life. I can't see him but I know he's there. If I have love and care and feeling, that's all I need. I've got faith. I have faith in Andrea — she's my life. I believe in her. I have faith in you, in everybody. Faith in God — it's the same thing — God is in people. If you don't have that, what've you got?

I was at a party not long ago, talking to a woman we know very well, and right out of the blue sky she says, "Jimmy, you should have been a preacher." And I told her, I says, "The last time I heard that was fifteen years ago when I was hanging out on street corners. Kids used to come to me with their problems. I guess I had a way of soothing them. 'Preacher Jim,' they called me." "Well," she says, "You just have a wonderful outlook on life." And I told her that I guess that's just the way I am. It's a little something special that God put in me, something extra he put in there, I guess. Maybe I was born with it. My father always had a nice outlook on life and my mother did, too. I hope my kids have it.

When I'm alone, I pray to God. Sometimes in bed or out fishing on the ice, I give him a thought. I say a little prayer to myself. Nobody hears it, just me. I don't tell people I do this thing. I don't get down on my hands and knees. I just think of what I'm going to do next in my life. I think of my boys and the girl. I think of my wife. I never ask God for anything, not even for good health. That's something you have to worry about yourself, but of course a little help from him I wouldn't mind. Most of the time I'm just thankful I'm alive and I have a family and I have a good job. If I prayed some other way, it just wouldn't be me.

Phil Welch

San Juan Island, Washington
May 7, 1974

Dear P.G.,

I don't know if my experience is typical of other young Christians who have "grown up" or "settled down." Many of the Christians I knew at the commune have taken completely different paths from mine. But I don't mind recalling the changes in my life as a Christian — in fact, I enjoy it — so I will try to answer your questions.

When I dropped out of Yale five years ago and moved to Everett, Washington, I knew that one segment of my life (call it my New England childhood and adolescence) had ended, but I had no idea what might come next. I spent a lot of time by myself those first three months thinking about where I had come from and where I was going, without any sense of a new direction. I had no friends there, I knew no one to talk to, but by chance, it seemed, I met a Christian who invited me to visit the commune where she lived. That was House of Emmanuel. On the day I left to go up there, I got a letter from Mom that said, "Dear Phil, here is a Psalm of David . . ." And then in parentheses she wrote, "Don't worry about the God part." What she meant was, "I know you're not religious but you might get something out of this." And it struck me then that I knew where I was going; there were so many coincidences that all seemed to lead toward the same idea, the idea that maybe God and religion were what were missing in my life.

When I arrived at House of Emmanuel, the people were outside working in the garden. The girl I knew introduced me and I worked with them for a little while. Then someone said, "You know we haven't prayed all morning?" And so they set down their shovels and rakes, made a circle and held hands, and prayed. It was so strange to me then — here were people like me praying and talking to God.

I knew that I would really like to give myself to the Lord like the Christians at House of Emmanuel, but I had a hard time believing that I could believe. My big fear was that, like everything else I had done before, this would be something I could begin but couldn't continue or finish. Part of me said this is it, this is really true, this is everything you've always needed, and the other part of me said you've gotta get out of here, this is the strangest thing you've ever been about to do. But finally someone gave me the confidence to believe that once you give yourself to God, he's there to keep you with it. It is his power, not your own, that supports your faith. I perceived it in a naive way then, but I realized that with God I wasn't alone, I wasn't struggling along on my own any more.

At House of Emmanuel there were just a few of us, ten or twenty at the most, who lived together and prayed together and followed the Lord. After several months there, I joined a Christian rock band and for the next year and a half that band was my life. We wrote songs about the Lord and played them at churches, schools, Christian coffeehouses, taverns, and rock festivals. It seemed like years, decades, so much happened in those months.

I met Sally in one of the Christian houses where we lived in Seattle. We were brother and sister for a long time in that house and another one outside of Seattle. But by the end of the summer of '70, we knew that we had much deeper feelings for each other. We got married in October.

You ask how I "decided" to go back to school and try to become a doctor. I don't know if I ever did decide that. It was something we talked about and prayed about for a long time. When I first left Yale, I intended never to go back to school, but after two or three years I started to wonder. I think what was in my mind was the parable of the talents: the servant who hid the one coin he was given was punished for not using it. Somehow that struck me personally, so I enrolled in classes at the University of Washington in September, 1971, just to see what it was like. I kept piling up the medical-school application requirements and just trusted the Lord to see if I would be accepted or rejected at the medical schools I applied to. I fantasized a career as a toymaker in case I didn't get in. But I did. I'll start this fall.

Did I think I was copping out by taking on an establishment role? If I had feelings like that, they came more from my old days at Yale than from values I shared with other young Christians. At House of Emmanuel we had thought about taking literally some of the things Jesus said like: "Give no thought to tomorrow, what ye shall eat and what ye shall put on, but consider the lilies of the field." Some people I knew really lived that way but they've all, I think, made a transition one way or another to taking some thought. It just didn't seem realistic to us not to provide for ourselves, especially with a baby coming, because if we didn't, we ended up depending on food stamps, on our families — it wasn't a holy walk, it felt more like irresponsibility. We felt, also, a need to be more involved with the concerns of the world and with our non-Christian friends. It seemed that there was more to being a Christian than just loving Jesus.

Yes, we're still aware of the presence of God in our lives, although it was really a lot easier to follow the Lord in a group of young Christians with newborn enthusiasms. In those days we thought, boy, just give me a chance to drop my nets and follow him. That was an easy way to go — easier than to stay at home with your nets and follow in spirit and still keep a simple kind of life together with a family and a job. Life at places like House of Emmanuel or the Lighthouse Ranch is different from ordinary reality. It makes possible experiences people wouldn't have otherwise, but to go on as a Christian really poses some questions. Our way of answering them is only one way.

We go to church, but not very often any more. We pray, we say grace at dinner, we read the Bible, we sing songs about the Lord. I don't know if there is a "right" way to live. I don't really think of it that way. Some people do. Some of the Christians we know don't think we're right and they feel they have the ability to say that about another person. We don't expect our next-door neighbors to bend themselves into a pattern of life like the one the Lord's handed us if it doesn't seem to fit them. That's not the way it should be. God is much, much bigger than that, I think.

Excluding a completely different treatment by fate, I don't think our lives would be much different if we hadn't become Christians. Sally and I are what we are. What the Lord is teaching us is to be truly forgiving. Before I was much more critical; it seemed perfectly logical to judge people. I think the way we make decisions would be different, too, if we weren't Christians. We would just be on our own, completely on our own. Our faith would be faith in our own wisdom, our own power — and I can see how you could really get to doubt that. Sally and I both have a kind of simple trust that if we make a wrong decision the Lord will turn us around and that somehow all things will work together to the good.

Do I have any spiritual goals? Look at Psalm 131. Sally has underlined that in five colors in our Bible. "My heart has no lofty ambitions, I am not concerned with marvels beyond my scope," it says. "It is enough for me to keep my soul tranquil and quiet." That's enough for us to strive for. We are blessed with Benjy and Lil — sometimes we wonder how our small family could be any happier.

I've answered your questions as if my life were done changing, but the most surprising thing I've found out about growing up is that the process doesn't stop. You didn't ask me if I am confused. I am, but one of the basic truths I have, which goes right back to how it all began for me as a Christian, is that the Lord is with us, he's teaching us, he's making us grow. When I have doubts, I ask him to show me the way and in his own fashion and in his own time, he does show me.

You asked if I thought God cares whether I want to share my life with him. Well, Philip, that's what he says he does; that's what it's all about for us. I don't think we want more involvement with God than he can give us. It's rather the other way around.

Come and see us soon, we'll roast you a salmon.

Love,
PHIL WELCH

VI　Gifts of the Spirit

Gifts of the Spirit

"I kept saying what if I ask him into my heart and he won't come into my heart? And they said, he will. And I said what if I've done too many bad things and he doesn't want me? And they told me that it says in the Bible, if you ask him in, he's going to come in. Finally I asked him to come into my heart and he did. I felt it. I knew it. I felt like a fountain had started in my stomach and bubbled all the way through my body. And I reached out and I touched something. I touched something solid. And I felt just like somebody hit me over the back of the head. All of a sudden I started speaking in a different language and I knew God was real. And from that time on no one could tell me God isn't real.

"And I just started crying. I thought, I may look dirty on the outside but, boy, I sure am clean on the inside." (CANDY, *Cucamonga, California*)

In the language of Pentecostalism, this is the Baptism of the Holy Spirit. It is idea becoming reality, a gift from God who is eternally ready to bestow it. One has only to ask in faith to receive this and other precious gifts, like new words of prayer, the power of healing, the gift of prophecy. These gifts are the "charismata"

"It's better felt than telt" —

MARVIN SCHMIDT

promised long ago to Christians by the Holy Spirit. They are the source of energy for the fastest growing religion in the United States.

Members of the Pentecostal movement trace its beginnings to the first manifestation of the Holy Spirit after the resurrection of Jesus:

"When Pentecost day came around they had all met in one room when suddenly they heard what sounded like a powerful wind from heaven, the noise of which filled the entire house in which they were sitting; and something appeared to them that seemed like tongues of fire; these separated and came to rest on the head of each of them. They were all filled with the Holy Spirit, and began to speak in foreign languages as the Spirit gave them the gift of speech." (ACTS *2:1–4*)

The gifts soon multiplied. St. Paul wrote of nine of them: the preaching of wisdom, the preaching of instruction, faith, healing, the power of miracles, prophecy, the recognition of spirits, the gift of tongues, and the interpretation of tongues. Eventually a reflection of Paul's own conversion experience was incorporated in the Pentecostal repertoire:

"Suddenly, while he was travelling to Damascus and just before he reached the city, there came a light from heaven all around him. He fell to the ground, and then he heard a voice saying, 'Saul, Saul, why are you persecuting me?'

" 'Who are you, Lord?' he asked, and the voice answered, 'I am Jesus . . .' " (ACTS *9:3–5*)

Some evangelists like Marvin Schmidt believe this incident is the prototype of what they call "slaying in the Spirit." At his revivals, Marvin prays over people and lays his hands on their heads. Suddenly, the manifest presence of God overwhelms them. They are felled to the carpet just as Paul was thrown to the dusty Damascus road. The power, Marvin insists, comes entirely from the Holy Spirit. He is merely one of God's agents.

After one of Marvin's revivals at the First Assembly of God Church in Pomona, California, I jotted this note in my journal:

"After the sermon, the evangelist asked anyone who wanted to be filled with the Holy Spirit to come forward and stand in front of the altar. Well, it takes a lot of guts to stand up and walk down front. I'm sure I would never have done it, but since I was sitting in the front row I didn't have to do anything. I didn't even have to stand up because we were all standing at that moment singing. So when the area near the platform became crowded with people, sixty or seventy of them, it looked as if I was one of those who had come up.

"The critical moment came when Marvin asked everyone not seeking prayer to sit down. Oh man . . . What do I do? Well, I'd been praying for a while and I decided I wanted to be filled with the Spirit and I really had to try.

"I closed my eyes at this point because I did not want to see Marvin approaching me. I knew I would flinch and ruin it all. I could hear Marvin slaying people on the other side of the church. This was scary enough, but not nearly as bad as the fact that occasionally it didn't work. Some people just didn't fall.

"Suddenly Marvin's hands were around my head. There was no pressure. Of course, my stomach felt as if it were coming up into my throat, but within seconds I was able to calm down. Then nothing happened.

"I just stood there with his hands on my head and he prayed over me in a quiet voice. I thought, oh, no, what am I going to do now, this is ridiculous. I don't feel a thing, what a disappointment. And then, at this most cynical moment, ZAP. I was swept off my feet and landed on the floor. No one pushed me, Marvin's hands had not moved, his voice had not altered. But I lost control of my body completely and I went down. I felt that I was swirling through infinite space, comforted and held in Jesus' arms. I felt nothing when I hit the floor.

"I lay on the floor unable to move. I shook and my mouth worked silently, shaping sounds but not out loud. Had I actually made the sounds, I would probably have been 'speaking in tongues.' I couldn't get up for half an hour."

For most people this experience founds a Christian life. In my case that just isn't the way it worked out. I didn't seek conversion, I didn't receive it. I did want, and still cherish, that remarkable brief knowledge of God's power (it remains one of the major events in my life) and I have no doubt in my mind that it came neither from Marvin himself nor from my own psychological feelings of the moment. The power was real and I lived in its bliss for days afterward.

True conversion, awareness, and acceptance of the power of Jesus Christ rarely requires as much evidence as "slaying in the Spirit." The Holy Spirit baptism can have the mildness of private prayer. It can be a gentle awakening to the immensity of God's love.

Often the setting is a prayer meeting. Plush living room armchairs are pulled closer to upholstered sofas, clanging church basement steel chairs are drawn together in a circle. Singing is followed by testimony from those who have already received the baptism. Those who are yet to receive it — sinners, ignorant of the love of Jesus — are urged to ask him into their hearts and to accept him as their personal savior. When an honest suppliant, brave with hope, asks aloud to receive the baptism, he is dazzled with the Spirit of Jesus. Elation and love swell within him. The shining mystery of Scripture stands transparent before him. He may speak in tongues immediately or seek that gift soon after. He may weep for joy. Like Candy, he feels clean and new. He is reborn.

The Spirit of the Lord works anywhere. Elder Rash of the Church of God in Christ of Sunflower, Mississippi, recalled his conversion: "I was coming along from the gin at Drew in the year '30, and I was hauling cotton with mules. The Spirit of the Lord began to work with me there and it just gave me the leap for joy right there in the wagon, coming along by myself. And so that's the way I received the Holy Ghost."

This blessing is never earned. The gifts of the Spirit are free. Like dry ice subliming, the believer is transformed from a state of ignorance to one of grace. Should he neglect his faith, should sin steal into his heart, he can be renewed. The Spirit can remind him

of its power and restore him to its glory.

Revivalism lacks the ubiquity of sin. From time to time, squalls of Pentecostalism stir the complacency of established religion and send ripples of enthusiasm to strike churches in all directions, but in the past little has remained at the points of origin.

Pentecostal churches, always idiosyncratic, evolve as their congregations change. With the exception of charismatic Catholics, Episcopalians and a few others, Pentecostal Christians mold their worship almost entirely from immediate personal experiences of the Holy Spirit and fundamentalist interpretations of Holy Scripture.

Evangelical leadership is itself a gift and not the least important one in the history of Pentecostalism. Some preachers do not merely conduct a congregation, they personify it. More than one church has been buried with its founder.

The gifts of the Spirit cannot be taught, they can only be grasped. Grasped with enthusiasm. No second generation is obliged to accept them when the enthusiasm has passed away.

Three styles of Pentecostalism predominate in the United States today: the conservative revivalism of fundamentalist congregations, which organized at the turn of the century; the dynamic, spontaneous manifestations of the gifts in independent offspring of these churches; and the recent appearance of the charismata in dogmatic churches as vital supplements to the traditional worship.

Ancestor to the first is the "frontier religion" of tent meetings and fiery preachers, musty canvas hot to the touch, a week's worth of dust powdered so fine by holy rolling that great blobs of sweat slide like marbles on top of it. Relics of the old-time religion persist in rural areas, especially in the South, and in city neighborhoods where country ways are preserved.

Its influence is obvious in the Churches of God in Christ, which are also called the Holiness churches. Unlike the black Baptist churches, whose services are sedate by comparison, these black "sanctified" congregations emphasize the Holy Spirit baptism over the traditional water baptism. Although they believe in and practice many of the same gifts of the Spirit as do other Pentecostal

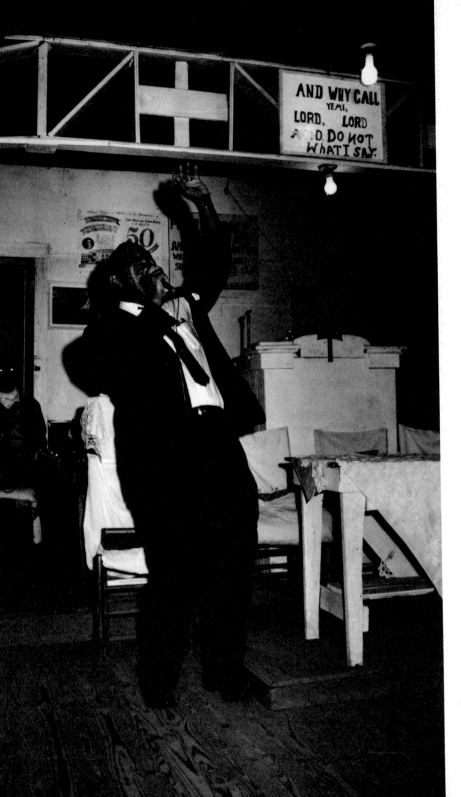

churches, both white and black, the Holiness churches possess an added dimension of intensity, not a reminder but an actual remnant of old-fashioned revival. Of all the church services I've ever been to, the revival at the Church of God in Christ of Sunflower, Mississippi was the most exhilarating.

It began with hymn singing, followed by the testimony of those who had been graced with an experience of God. The service, thoroughly spontaneous, seemed almost to have been orchestrated and choreographed. As one testimony ended, a song would begin, first as a quiet hum under the conclusion of the testimony, then rising in intensity until a new testimony interrupted it.

Finally nearly everyone had spoken and the sermon began. Every sentence was greeted by voices shouting, "Amen," "Thank you, Lord!" (On several occasions I've spoken to an audience accustomed to responding in this manner. It makes speaking a pleasure. You feel that the crowd is with you. It encourages you to keep at it, give it all you've got.)

As the responses encouraged him, the preacher at Sunflower started moving as he talked, vibrating with energy, communicating excitement. "The Holy Spirit is in this church!" The congregation couldn't sit any longer. They stood up and began singing, then dancing. I was virtually swept up in the frenzy which enveloped the dancers. I danced at Sunflower because it was the only way I could keep up with the movement well enough to photograph it. I danced because I couldn't sit still.

The heat was overwhelming. Sweat poured from our faces. The confines of the tiny church seemed inadequate to the enormous energy. Yet nothing seemed to dampen the fervor. Finally, several people were knocked down by the power of the Lord and a long period of quiet prayer concluded the service. The next day I couldn't recall everything that had happened. It was as if during the high moments of the revival I had lost touch with myself, as if it weren't really happening to me.

Rosalie, whose dancing that night surpassed everyone else's, later gave me her testimony:

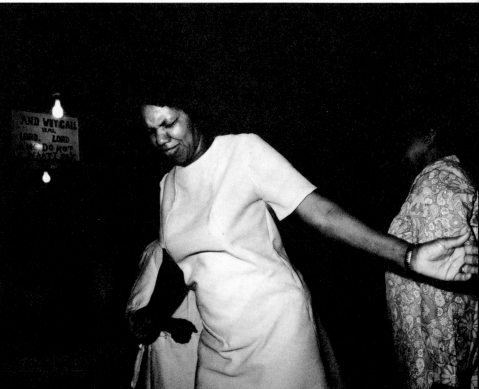

"The night I came back from up North, about four hours after I was here, my father passed away. I felt that it was the Spirit of God that had directed me to come back home.

"Even so, I disobeyed the Spirit of God. I was kind of like Jonah when he was trying to get away from the Lord and instead of me joining up with the church, I went and started running a cafe.

"And I guess I run it about a year and I didn't have no complaints. But after that my conscience began to worry me and I could hear a voice — seemed like whispering in my ear. Somebody would talk to me saying, 'blessed is the man walketh not in the counsel of the ungodly.'

"And when two of my brothers were praying for my grandmother something spoke to me then and said, 'that's what you should be doing but you're not fittin to do.' Right then and there I made up my mind that I wanted to be holy. And that Sunday I went to church.

"The whole while I was in the service I was saying to myself, 'Lord, fill me with your Holy Spirit.' During the testimony time I got up and I began to say, 'I thank God for being here,' and that is just about all that I remember saying because the Spirit of God moved on me. It knocked me out and I rolled on the floor. I knew it was the Spirit of God. I could hear the song saying, 'I'm free at last.'

"Later my brother told me, 'Oh, you spoke in tongues today. You really spoke in tongues. The Lord has filled you with his precious Holy Ghost.' And I said, 'Thank you, Jesus.' "

In the mid-twentieth century, a second surge of renewal caused many old charismatic churches which had lost their vigor to rebound dramatically. Small groups broke away from the more established congregations to form powerfully gifted prayer meetings and independent Pentecostal churches began to spring up in suburbs and in cities.

One of these is the Faith Tabernacle Church in Riverside, California, where a small but rapidly growing congregation shares an enthusiastic worship. The services at Faith Tabernacle are thoroughly unpredictable. I remember wanting to learn what was going

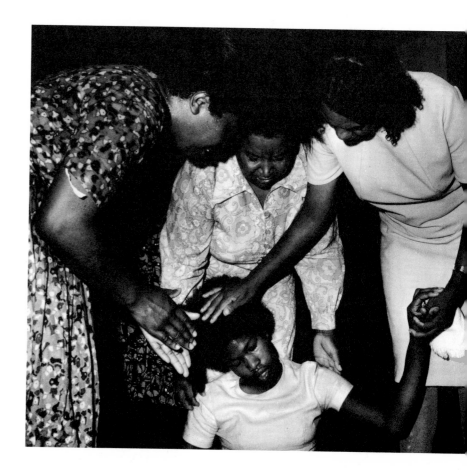

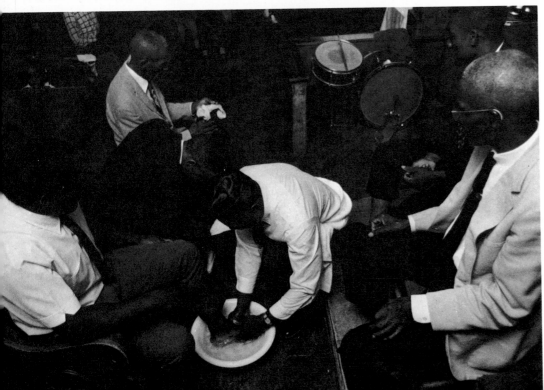

Jesus washed his disciples' feet and told them if I am your Lord and master and I wash your feet, then you should wash one another's feet. Because it's the lowest part of an individual's body and usually people that would shake your hand, they wouldn't bother your feet. It's a manner of condescending one with another and it makes us feel together as one.

REVEREND SCOTT

I went down to a revival and heavy as I am the Lord used me and I moved my feet. (At Church of God in Christ, Itta Benna, Mississippi)

to happen the night we filmed there. Rev. Pat Yarbrough, the Pastor, told me he didn't know and wouldn't until it happened. It's "as the Lord moves." On the night we filmed, the Lord moved abundantly.

The excitement started with the song service. It was so rousing that an elderly woman in the front row jumped to her feet and began dancing, alone, carried not just by the beat of the music but by the Spirit of the Lord. As she later explained, "It's just another manifestation of his Spirit. It's an exuberance, it's just a lifting up of the Spirit. It gets in your feet and someone else is moving your feet besides you!"

Across the room a young woman named Judy played the organ, sang, and waved her hands up to the Lord all at one time: "I use the organ because this is my position. This is what I do for the Lord. When I'm up here I ask him, Lord, love me. And just let me touch tonight, if nothing else, the hem of your garment. Just let me feel a witness that you're here, right now. Right at this organ. Not with maybe somebody greater than I, but just with somebody like me, an everyday, average person who loves you with all her heart. And I do . . ."

Eventually, Pat Yarbrough entered from the back of the church, dressed in a red suit with white patent leather shoes. In a sultry voice, a reminder of his days as a night-club singer, he sang a song he had just written. And then he gave a fiery sermon:

"What we need now are the real, genuine, Holy Ghost filled men and women who have truly confidence in the Lord. Confidence in him? What do you mean confidence, preacher? Confidence that whatever he said he will do, he will do it.

"Oh, I know that sometimes it's hard even to have confidence in our economy, sometimes it's hard to have confidence in each other, sometimes it's hard to have confidence in flesh. But if we could have the confidence that God wants us to have in him, we could receive a miracle. We could receive a blessing. We could receive salvation. We could receive the Baptism of the Holy Spirit with the evidence, speaking in other tongues."

I remember, coming home one evening, well, I was about half tight, drunk, and I thought it would be a very gentlemanly thing to go pick mother up at church in my car.

So I went down to the little mission on Broadway in Los Angeles and I thought the service would be over. But when I got there the preacher had just stepped to the pulpit for the message of the evening. So I sat there on the back seat and the longer he preached, the more sense he made to me. And before it was over with, he certainly convinced me that I needed salvation.

Here was a drunk boy going to the altar and God was so kind. He so gloriously saved me, filled me with the Spirit, sobered me up, and I took mother home that night with a completely different attitude than I thought I would be taking her home. That was my conversion. And at the age of twenty I was pastoring a large church.

REVEREND YARBROUGH

I love Jesus like I do my husband, like I love my
mother. Many times when I'm afraid and alone, sad,
broken-hearted, I just tell him how much I love him
and that seems to make everything all right.

JUDY

Suddenly Judy, who had moved to the pews to listen to the sermon, rose from her seat and began to speak in tongues. The strange sounds were loud and packed with feeling and, although incomprehensible, deeply moving. There was complete silence when she finished.

Then Reverend Yarbrough called out, "Somebody obey the Lord!"

A man rose from his seat and with the same intensity which had gripped Judy, spoke in English. The Lord gave him the interpretation of the words Judy had previously spoken:

"The Lord said, my children do not despair, I love thee at this hour.

"I come to thee in compassion and understanding regarding your trials, the problems that are set before thee.

"I have come to thee, that you shall have comfort, that all things shall be done justly and in order.

"Weep before the Lord and you shall know the compassion that I have for you."

Talking about the experience in an interview later, Judy explained it very simply: "Well, what I'm doing is I'm talking to Jesus. That's what it is. And only he and I . . . only he and I know what's going on. And when prophecy comes forth the meaning is revealed. But there's something . . . I don't even know if I can tell you. If that camera could see into my heart, even now, and into my bones, and in my fingers and know that this Spirit, this Holy Ghost lives in me, this Jesus. And that when it comes, it becomes so strong in my being, it even makes me smile."

After the sermon, Reverend Yarbrough invited those who desired to be prayed for to step forward. At first people hesitated, unlike the great rush at Marvin Schmidt's revival. When the first man came forward Yarbrough prayed for him at some length with one hand on the man's head. At the critical moment Yarbrough's inflection changed and the man went down.

"When a proper man comes into the experience, or into the presence of the almighty God," explains Yarbrough, "it pretty well

just buckles his knees and he can't stand in the presence of God. As far as being mental, or as far as blacking out or as far as anything physically harmful is concerned, there's none of that at all. It's just that people just can't stand the presence of God that strong."

Soon the front of the church was mobbed with people coming up to be prayed for. Many others lay on the floor shaking and speaking in tongues, while still more people bent over them and prayed with them. "The hand of God is moving faster now," exclaimed Yarbrough, moving quickly from one person to another, slaying them as fast as they could come forward. "Everyone come, God wants to fill you full of the Holy Ghost." "Come in eagerness and faith." ZAP. "It takes the worry out of a heart, just raise your hands up." ZAP. "Get ready man." ZAP. "Lord let this girl have more than just a shallow life. Give her power. Give her glory. Give her . . ." ZAP. "Oh, glory, glory, glory."

"When people come to me for prayer, if they really want prayer, then I pray for 'em," says Yarbrough. "Now it's not that I yell or holler or whoop or jump or anything like that. But I put faith behind it. I put feeling behind it. And I release my faith to them. And ninety percent of the time it knocks the props out from under 'em."

While many come forward on their own, Yarbrough occasionally points to someone, and orders him up. He says the Lord makes him notice that a man or woman has a special problem and needs healing. Often it's someone who wanted to share in the experience but didn't have the will to take the first bold step. Mike was one: "Reverend Yarbrough called me out of the crowd and said would I come forward and I did. At that moment when he laid his hand on me, I fell backward. I was conscious. I could recall things going on around me. But yet it seemed as if God was ministering to my spirit while I was in this state as I fell back. As the guys say, I got zapped."

Even after having been "zapped" myself at Marvin Schmidt's revival I found the service at Pat Yarbrough's church amazing. The sheer amount of energy released in that room had a myriad of effects: many of us were carried away with laughter and giggling; others were crying, screaming, or fervently singing.

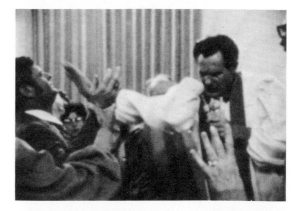

The atmosphere is different at King's Temple in Seattle, Washington. Even among Pentecostal churches, King's Temple seems bizarre. Its pastor is a female prophet, Charlotte Baker. She is one of a group of associated ministers who have received the gift of prophecy.

The purpose of prophecy is to reveal God's will. When an individual receives it, the prophecy can lead him toward a career, or relieve him of doubt about his present occupation, whether spiritual or mundane. It foretells what his role will be in the Kingdom of God on earth.

It is necessary for the prophesying minister to be a stranger to his or her subject, so on several occasions each year Rev. Baker invites one or two of her colleagues to come to Seattle. The visiting ministers, who do not know her congregation, pray over those who wish to receive this particular guidance and prophesy their future. Reverend Baker does the same in other churches. To illustrate God's purpose in the revelation, the prophet relates incidents from the individual's past (known only through divine intuition) to events in his future. Prophecy is also given for the entire body of the church, and it is used to appoint leaders.

King's Temple has received another extraordinary gift in addition to prophesy: singing in tongues. The phenomenon begins with people speaking in tongues, itself an unnerving sound for the unfamiliar. Some voices warble, others drone, all in different rhythms. Instrumental music is added and the voices begin to harmonize these strange utterances from God. The result is an eerie, high-pitched, hollow sound which reverberates throughout the large church.

Many, many churches like Faith Tabernacle and King's Temple have grown suddenly since the late sixties. Their congregations have swelled with young people, especially those who have turned away from the "hippie" drug culture to find Jesus. For the first time, many of them discover a being who really loves them, individually and forever. The vitality and the immediacy of Pentecostal religion is so strong that it seizes them completely.

In their exuberance, some young evangelists are intolerant not only of "sinners" but of other Christians as well. Others who perform slayings in the Spirit and attract large crowds to their revivals suffer episodes of absent-mindedness about the real source of the power behind their extraordinary gifts. The lessons of humility seemed lost on one young preacher I met in California. When I asked him for a personal statement for my tape recorder, he blistered me with a sermon on the horrors of Hell and relentless power of Satan. My dog Charlie, waiting nearby in my truck, chose this moment to begin barking in his own irritating and relentless way. "In the name of Jesus, I rebuke that dog!" cried out the young evangelist. Charlie was still barking half an hour later when the young man drove away in his white Lincoln Continental.

This is not to suggest that most young Christians lack humility. (That frailty belongs to a minority of Christians who are "young" in the Lord, not necessarily in age.) Pride is merely a small side effect of the explosive growth and enthusiasm of the Pentecostal movement. The extraordinary warmth of the Lighthouse Ranch exemplifies the love of the young Christian movement.

The most significant feature of Pentecostalism today is the fact that it is no longer confined to a certain type of church or a certain form of worship. "Charismatic prayer" and the "Baptism of the Holy Spirit" are becoming known and practiced in an increasing number of conservative, traditional churches. Many priests and pastors have recognized the gifts as valid, indeed powerful, experiences of God, which are available to anyone who wishes to seek them. Others view them as a threat to their form of worship, as emotional excesses devoid of religious value.

Pentecostalism has divided more than one family. At a prayer meeting in Spokane I met a woman who had recently received the Baptism of the Holy Spirit. Quite typically her children had experienced it before she did and it was a credit to her open-mindedness that she had allowed them to lead her to a new life. Beaming with the radiance that comes from the baptism, she pointed out two kids in the room and told me they were also her "children." She had "adopted" them because their parents, strict members of a

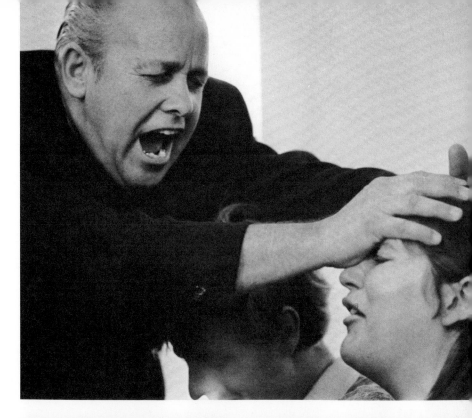

Charismatic prayer meetings take place in private houses as well as in churches. At this one in Seattle, the leader has received the gift of healing and prays for his friends.

denominational church, had denounced the Pentecostal experience and made life at home miserable for them. So happy was she to have received the baptism and so grateful for the opportunity to show her love, she failed to see the tragedy of the situation.

Nowhere is the conflict more evident than in the Catholic Pentecostal movement. Among Catholics who are used to rote prayers, elaborate ritual, private confession, and minimal personal participation, the qualities of Pentecostalism provide a sharp contrast and, for some, tremendous fulfillment. In others, Pentecostalism provokes only condemnation and fear. (Certainly the sight and sound of a nun in full habit praying loudly in the language of the Holy Spirit can be a bit disconcerting the first time around.) Catholic Pentecostals stress that the gifts of the Holy Spirit are just that, gifts, which contribute to the totality of the Catholic faith and thereby enrich it.

Father Fulton of Seattle exemplifies the spirit-filled Catholic clergy. After the Second Vatican Council ended the Latin Mass, Father Fulton began to "die on the vine," and even to doubt the reality of Jesus Christ. He responded to the early charismatic awakenings in the church with suspicion, while remarking the joyful radiance of those who were part of the movement. As he became better acquainted with charismatic Christians, both Catholic and Episcopal, he lost his apprehension and received the Baptism of the Holy Spirit.

"I was trying to pray for someone in need, my own priest, a brother in need and the Lord gave me a tongue to pray with and this . . . I call it release of the Holy Spirit. And from then on my life has been entirely changed. I didn't realize it at first but I found that from then on I had a tremendous power of love within me.

"Young people started coming into our church and they said to me, 'Why Father Fulton, don't you realize the Mass is so boring to us, couldn't you let us have a guitar Mass?' I'd been horrified by such a thought before and I said, 'Why, of course. Yes.' So I had my young children start a guitar Mass. The first Mass we celebrated was so beautiful, so full of praise and thanksgiving and joy and love that by the time it was over I was practically dancing. I just cried out, 'Praise the Lord!' to the congregation because my whole life, my prayer life, seemed suddenly to become full of praise and thanksgiving.

"After receiving the Holy Spirit, I realized to my intense joy and relief that Jesus Christ is real and that he's risen today. That it's all true. I saw him living in people's lives all around me. I saw people coming from death into life constantly and that's what I'd done, because I'd been in such an awful state, I just couldn't relate to all the new ways and different things happening in the Church and suddenly I was relating to everybody. I just loved them and the love kept flowing."

The charismatic movement has even touched some monasteries. At the Trappist monastery in Vina, California, charismatically inclined monks lead a weekly prayer meeting open to visitors. The meeting itself is quite subdued, but several monks have or still do pray in tongues.

In Pecos, New Mexico, an entire brotherhood of monks has been baptized in the Holy Spirit. Our Lady of Guadalupe Benedictine Abbey is the first Catholic Pentecostal abbey in the country. It is a center for spiritual renewal and offers charismatic retreats for families and clergy throughout the year. Father Scully of Pecos discussed the charismatic movement:

"When I first heard about this Pentecostal thing, I was open to it. I couldn't see why if something happened in the first century it wouldn't happen in the twentieth, if that's the way God wanted to work. But when it came to the point of actually getting involved myself, then there was a great deal of trepidation.

"The other monks invited me to a dinner where they were going to pray over people after the meal. I went more or less to see what it was all about, not to get involved in it. I had never prayed that way before, you know. Spontaneous prayer never, and certainly not in tongues.

"I was on the margin of the whole thing, watching, praying my own way — silently — not knowing what to do. And then after a while I said, well, I think I'll just try it. And there were funny words there so I just kept saying them and then there came a kind of pleasure with the whole thing, a delight, an awareness of God. The next day I felt tremendous happiness and unbelievable peace — a cloud-nine type of thing. It's hard even to describe it.

"And then by using the gift of tongues as prayer over a span of time, I became convinced that it was prayer. Because I find that whenever I'm in deepest union with God, I shift into tongues. The Baptism in the Spirit, as it's called, confirmed the validity of the religious life and the monastic life. It gave meaning and practicality to most of the things we were doing, the basic elements of our life.

"At Pecos, we began to incorporate Pentecostal elements into our way of life. We are trying to form a synthesis between Pentecostal spirituality and traditional monastic spirituality. We introduce people to the Pentecostal movement and try to help them open themselves up to the gifts that the Spirit is offering at this time."

What the Spirit is offering at this time is proof, proof that things are not what they are, and especially not what they seem, in the realm of power, human and divine. It is difficult to be both "objective" and unambiguous, but it seems presumptuous to assume automatically that speaking in tongues or being slain in the Spirit are instances of mass hypnosis or hysteria. From my personal experience and from many conversations with others who have received the gifts of the Spirit, I am convinced that they are moments when a human being experiences the absolute connection between himself and the forces which are part of the cosmos.

The gifts of the Spirit offer immediate physical evidence, accessible even to the most skeptical intellectual, of God's particular love. They can bring about healing or conversion, they can awaken a newcomer to a realm he has not explored, but best of all they improve with translation into daily use. People change. As Father Fulton puts it, they are brought from death into life. They learn how to give love by receiving it. Surely it would be a foolish mistake to dismiss the gifts of the Spirit as mere emotionalism. Pentecostalism is indeed rich in emotion, but, like love itself, it grows from roots deep in our being.

VII   Louise

Louise

TOMMY TAYLOR:

This is Louise, a very small town. We say it's the best little small town
in the county. My father, my mother, my brothers always live around
Louise. They all passed away now and left me here in Louise. It's
just a nice place to live.

We have some nice people that live in Louise. They people that
you can depend on. Not everybody live well. Plenty of people living
around Louise unfortunate. When you're unfortunate, there's nothing much we can do about it. We all have to harden up and go along
with it. Everyone doesn't get the blessing alike.

Jesus said, "You shall have trials and tribulations. In me you
have peace." Jesus had a hard time while he was in this world. He
went from the cross on by the grave. He stayed in the grave two days
and two nights and on the third day he rose. In that period of time,
Jesus had a hard time. And all of us that followed after Jesus, we
must have a hard time. We must go through the same ordeal Jesus
went through. Death occurs in our families. We must harden up.
We must learn to take it. It breaks us down. It leaves us screaming
and hollering. But Jesus cried out loud on the cross and give up the
ghost. So all of his followers must have trials, must have tribula-

When I was baptized I went down to the water and when I went down there I felt like a new man. Come up feeling good. I feels that way now. Everytime I get talking about it I feel good. I feel like I did then. I never will forget that day when the Lord laid his hands on me.

PENNY BARNES

Whenever anybody goes in the water and take on the faith of baptism, he feels like he has been born over. From then on he lives a new life. He don't live the same old life no more. Because the same old life has been did away with. Other person that hasn't been regenerated and born again, he can't act like we act. He doesn't have nothing within. Whenever you been changed from death unto life, it put the new life in you.

TOMMY TAYLOR

tions, must serve him by the way of the cross.

Look at Pearla Mae Franklin. Pearla Mae's parents died seven or eight years ago. Pearla Mae did the best she could, helping take care of her fourteen brothers and sisters. She kept the house clean. She kept the food ready for those that was going to school. She did the ironing and the washing and all. Very hard with no mother and no father in the house.

But Pearla Mae didn't let that be none of her problem because she feel like if God did it — it were right. She just goes along and do the best she can over the family conditions and don't let it worry her. That's what makes people strong in their faith. They don't worry about things. That's the way Pearla Mae sees it. She says God did it and she just takes it and goes ahead on.

Now, Penny Barnes used to be a tenant farmer. Eventually he made up in his mind to buy some land of his own. Him and his wife put their shoulders together over the years and now they own 30 acres of land. They weren't fortunate enough to have a family.

Penny Barnes is a tough and stout man. He is a man that you can depend on. Anytime you need him it doesn't get too dark or don't get too cold. Penny believe in helping less fortunate people. He feels like he's justified toward God when he lives that kind of life. Just the kind of a life the Lord requires out of everybody.

PENNY BARNES:

I live a Christian life and I'm rich. Rich in God. Everything I need, he got. Everything I've got belongs to him. He says whenever I want to ask for anything with faith, he grant it to me. You ain't got nothin' to worry about when you living for God. Not a thing. He supply your needs. You know, we may want some things we don't need, but he supply the needs. It ain't never fail.

God told man to till the soil and live off the sweat of his eyebrow. That means he has got to work in the field. That's what he told man to do. Get out there and till the soil and make a living for his family. So I don't mind none doin' it cause I'm doin' what God say to do. When I'm pickin' cotton I think about how good the

If you is converted you find yourself praying. You can't get along without prayer. Do you think God would come up to you and offer you something without you asking him?

LIZZIE LINNEAR

*I get a kick out of being a Christian, yeah. If you live right God's gonna give you something to do. **That's the way he work.** You tell him you want to do more for him every day of your life and he give you something. That's right.*

PENNY BARNES

Penny Barnes is a man of his word. He found out that a man's word is his barn and his barn is his security.

TOMMY TAYLOR

179

Lord is to me. If it weren't for him I wouldn't be able to do it. All the health and strength come from God.

TOMMY TAYLOR:

Lizzie Linnear is a good woman, Christian woman. She doesn't take sides with nobody but the Lord. Anybody in the community has the misfortune to be sick, she believe in going in there and finding out what they need. That's what we call religion in our state. We are concerned about each other. She believes in her heart about God. That he is a God that will save her according to her faith.

PENNY BARNES:

Lizzie Linnear? She's a Christian woman. Love to work. She live by herself in the time of the flood. After the water come last spring she didn't even move out. She stayed right there. The water got right up to the house, but she stayed right there and just before the water come she ran out and God stopped it. Backed it up. She stayed right there in that water by herself. She got plenty faith in God. Plenty of it.

LIZZIE LINNEAR:

I live all by myself out here. I likes it out here by myself. I don't have anybody to upset me, disturb my mind. I always keep a satis-fied mind.

I don't feel lonely, I feel the Spirit here at home. The Holy Spirit . . . Some nights I don't go to bed. I sit up here and sing and play music by myself and the Spirit will be right here with me.

When we had the flood, I stayed right here in this house. I didn't give it no thought to go into town. I just said the Lord is here just like he was in town. He'll take care of me here, and he did do it. I didn't leave. There ain't but one thing goin' to carry me away from back here. That's when my last day comes. I go. I think it's a hymn says, "Death can't make my soul afraid if God be with me then," and I always know that he'll be with me because I'm surely converted.

You got to let your life be your light. And when you let your life be your light, the spirit can come in and you can feel it. If I'm acting right I feel the Spirit. Acting wrong, I don't feel no spirit. The Spirit won't dwell in an unclean temple.

LIZZIE LINNEAR

181

How I feel about God? The way I feel about God, God is a spirit. The only way we can deal with God, we must get in the spirit as he is. When the spirit hits the individual he's a changed person. It works like fire. It burns him inside. Sometimes you feel like screaming and hollering when you in the spirit with God.

I'm a part of God. God created the heaven and the earth and the fire and the air and the beasts and the sea and whatnot. Then he said, "Let us make man in our image, in the likeness of us." So God cut the dust from the earth and made man. So man is made in the image of God. That's why he's rejoicing.

TOMMY TAYLOR

When you got Jesus . . . you're rich. When you is converted and working with the Holy Spirit, that's where you're riches come from in keeping God's command and walking in his stature daily. And don't let worldly things, things of the world — you don't let that worry you. That's where your riches come from. It comes from God. And so when God sends somebody to you, you shouldn't turn them away, cause you don't know who you're turning away. So when he send somebody to me, I always smiles and let them know that Jesus is in me and I'm in him. I'm just wrapped up in Jesus.

LIZZIE LINNEAR

TOMMY TAYLOR:

Death is invisible. Nobody can see him. You don't know when he steps in the room. You don't know when he go out. You can have all the doors locked. Doesn't matter how close they're locked. How hard they're locked. Death gets in there some kind of way. He don't make no noise. He just tips on in the room. We haven't yet found out what he does to the sick person. We don't know whether he touches him or just looks at him or wink an eye at him. But we do know this. Whatever he does he doesn't have to do it but one time.

This life is just a type of shadow we're passing through. But the life we're concerned about is on the other side. We're not poor, we're rich. We feel rich because we have salvation of God in us. We can live with him throughout eternity on the other side. But you got to make preparations to inherit the life on this side. If we live right and trust God for his word we will inherit eternal life which will last as long as God reigns. That's the life we're concerned about.

LIZZIE LINNEAR:

When my little boy got killed I mourned a little bit over that, but afterward the Lord consolated me. I knows that I'm part of God cause he takes care of me. All I get, it comes from the Lord. Even to the breath I breathe, it belongs to the Lord and he just loans it to me for awhile. And when he get ready for it and when it's time for the house, this body here, when time for this house to dissolve, this breath is going back to God where it come from. Cause you know he made man, and when he made man he breathed in his nostrils the breath of life, and he became a living soul and when that breath goes away he's a dead soul. He just layin' there dead. And the body just laying there and his soul where God breathed into his nostrils has gone back to God.

This whole universe belongs to God and he just lets us stay here for awhile to use his land. We can't say it's ours, and nobody else can say it's ours. It belongs to God, and that's why I gives my service to the Lord because it's all his'n.

I been goin' through this land a long time. I been goin' out healin' people. I just go to them if they have a pain anywhere about them. I take my hand and lay it on 'em and pray to God and they be healed. He did healin'. It wasn't me. The power wasn't in my hand . . . in me. I was just lettin' him use me as his servant.

God don't want us to lay aside everything and not do nothing for the people. He put us here to serve the people. And when we serve the people we serve the Lord.

LIZZIE LINNEAR

List of Photographs